*K*nave, *F*ool, and *G*enius

Knave, Fool, and Genius

The Confidence Man as He Appears
in Nineteenth-Century American Fiction

by Susan Kuhlmann

The University of North Carolina Press
Chapel Hill

Library of Congress Cataloging in Publication Data

Kuhlmann, Susan, 1942–
  Knave, fool, and genius.

  Bibliography: p.
  1. American fiction—19th century—History and
criticism. 2. Deception in literature. I. Title.
PS377.K8   813'.009'352   73–493
ISBN 0–8078–1208–0

Manufactured in the United States of America
Printed by Heritage Printers, Inc.
ISBN–0–8078–1208–0
Library of Congress Catalog Card Number 73–493

For my mother and father

Contents

Preface

This study is the result of a longstanding affection for Melville coupled with hesitation in accepting the role of a "Melville-ist." Or a Hawthorne-ist or a Twain-ist. In my own case, I have found a lack of congeniality in the usual relationship between the critic and the author whom he adopts for the purposes of a temporary—or a lifelong—exercise of scholarship. The result of this kind of association is normally the scholarship of reconstituted reality, based on the facts of the real world in which Melville, Hawthorne, and Twain coexist. Without this kind of investigation, of course, literary criticism would be bankrupt; furthermore, the debts that one owes such scholars are beyond calculation. This work, however, is an attempt at what might be called the scholarship of reconstituted fiction, based on the qualities of the fictional world in which, for example, Ishmael and Coverdale coexist. It is obvious that such a fictional world is neither that of *Moby-Dick* nor that of *The Blithedale Romance*; rather, it is a hypothesis that comes into being for a short time as a result of the projection of the critic's mind over, let us say, the field of nineteenth-century American literature.

Perhaps the ideal, of which this study is only a first approximation, is the sustaining of a critical perspective within a narrative context in which the personae are the fictional characters of a period or a fashion of literary endeavor. The relationship thus established between critic and author would be a less formal one. It would seem to have the potential for mediating more successfully between the appreciative interest of the fiction lover and the private world of the fiction maker.

The differences between the two kinds of scholarship are perhaps less apparent in the subject matter than in the approach to it, although it has indeed seemed to me that the confidence man invites one to deal with him as a coconspirator. He is a fictional character who deals in fictions, and it is easy to respond in kind by inducing a quintessential confidence man and endowing him with a "real" existence as a literary phenomenon. And in fact I have come to accept some such hypothetical character as my protagonist. I have seen him as playing a number of roles, as being reincarnated in various forms which reveal the special qualities of each author who tricks him out in a new disguise. I have found that his equivocal nature places him at the right hand of creators who face their own moral and aesthetic dilemmas in handling the art of illusion. Thus, despite my tendency to treat the con man with the familiarity of a creator toward his creation, he has always chastened me with the vigor of his claim to be taken seriously and the proof of his appeal to the nineteenth-century American imagination. After all, he has been taken seriously by Hawthorne, Melville, Howells, Twain, and James. In the end I have had to accept him on his own terms as an oracular figure, although not forgetting that he is, after all, a fiction.

Among those who have read and shown interest in the initial stages of this project, I should like to thank William M. Gibson for his advice and encouragement. At the same time, I wish to free him from the imputation of consent to all of the later twists that have been given to the original conception. I should also like particularly to acknowledge the help of the librarians in charge of the sections on American literature in the New York Public Library and the special collections of the New York University Library.

Knave, Fool, and Genius

The Confidence Man

Under other names, the confidence man is an old subject in English literature, appearing in the form of certain characters so familiar and so inseparable from the kind of villainy they practice that their names are almost synonyms for it. Indeed, so early is the confidence man that he arrives on horseback in the fourteenth century. In one instance he is a devious Canon, preying on the gold lust and alchemy fever of a simpleminded priest. By means of a rigged experiment and protestations of good faith, Chaucer's Canon induces the priest to pay good money for a worthless formula, guaranteed to turn lesser metals into gold. A crabbed and eager fiend, he is one type of confidence man who has counterparts in the mining country of the American West. But Chaucer also gives us another kind, a genial, beardless teller of tales and vendor of relics, with a fixed aversion to manual labor. He is amusingly and contemptuously superior in his knowledge of human nature, and frankly enjoys his power to please the ear, the eye, and the credulous soul. The Pardoner is a good-humored rogue who is excellent company. His gifts become the inheritance of crowd-pleasing hypocrites on New England platforms, on backwoods stumps, in prairie tents, and in gambling dens.

But the confidence man is not merely venial, not always shallow. There are great precedents for the falsifiers of trust who are corruptive by nature and whose trickery is an expression of an abstract evil. There is of course the smiling villain Iago, breathing a malignancy so essential to his being that he has been thought to resemble the Vice in a morality play. Yet as an archhypocrite he is second to the Archfiend. Confidence won on false pretenses and in the lapse of better judgment is the Devil's achievement in Paradise. The Fall is in fact an archetype of the confidence game, and thus any successful game reminds us of congenital folly. In Milton's Satan, the Adversary of God, there is precedent for the use of the confidence man in the most serious of moral contexts. Thus, when an observer in Melville's *Confidence-Man* asks pointedly, "How much money did the devil make by gulling Eve?"[1] he recognizes the existence of gratuitous evil—and puts the confidence man back into a primordial drama of man and his gods.

While it is certainly true that the writers of fiction in early America knew Shakespeare and Milton, it is more important that they were conscious of being American rather than English, and of being only recently so. Native experience made them familiar with the canny treachery by which the Indian sometimes survived his contact with the white man. Indeed, one of the first confidence games that appears in our imaginative literature is a white man's adaptation of an Indian ruse. Teague, the Irish Sancho Panza who figures in H. H. Brackenridge's *Modern Chivalry* (1792–1815), is approached by confidence men who want to hire him to pose as an Indian chief. They will "introduce" him to government agents who will give him money and gifts to secure a peace treaty with his "people." The crude hoax has some of Twain's bizarre humor, inspired by an aroused social conscience, but it is one of the early, random instances which fall outside the scope of the present study. My own starting point will be the one from which it is possible to think of New England as "old" and Kentucky as "new." From here I shall go on to consider a number of appearances of the confidence man in nineteenth-century American fiction, giving some consideration to the context in which he is seen and waiving a strict chronology in order to group together examples related in type or in treatment.

Who, then, is the confidence man? Professor Johannes Dietrich Bergmann has shown that the term "confidence man" may have been applied first to a particular swindler caught in New York

1. Herman Melville, *The Confidence-Man: His Masquerade*, ed. Hershel Parker (New York: W. W. Norton & Company, 1971), p. 28.

City on July 7, 1849.[2] In an article entitled "The Original Confidence Man," Professor Bergmann describes the public interest aroused in the case of William H. Thompson. He also shows that contemporary accounts noted the larger significance of the con man; almost at once it was observed that a trickster who asked for and received "confidence" revealed much about the society that confided in him. The article brings together evidence that Melville was thinking of this particular confidence man when he created Frank Goodman in *The Confidence-Man: His Masquerade* (1857). For the more general purposes of this study, however, we must recognize that Thompson himself belonged to a category broader than the one he established by the peculiar features of his "confidence" game. We shall have to think of the confidence man as anyone whose profession it is systematically and deliberately to seek the confidence of another or others with the intention of abusing it for financial advantage. Occasionally this study will deal with individuals who are not, strictly speaking, members of the profession, but who practice it under unusual circumstances, as the man who designs his own house may be said to appropriate the role of the architect. Hence, Mark Twain's "Duke of Bridgewater" is a professional confidence man, while James's Kate Croy is a formidable amateur. As these examples indicate, the range of characters is immense. Since my subject is not the confidence man as a sociological phenomenon but as a literary one, I have not tried to be exhaustive in recording his appearances in the public records or subliterary fiction of the period. Nor have I thought it necessary to canvass the entire field of minor works which properly belong to the category of nineteenth-century American fiction. Such an attempt would have to take account, for example, of the brief gambling sequences in Poe's story "William Wilson" and of such longer but peripheral works as S. Weir Mitchell's *Autobiography of a Quack* (1900). Rather, it is my purpose to call attention to the fact that the confidence man is a character developed at length by certain "standard" authors, such as Hawthorne in *The Blithedale Romance*, Howells in *The Leather-*

2. Johannes Dietrich Bergmann, "The Original Confidence Man," *American Quarterly* 21 (Fall 1969): 561.

wood God, Mark Twain in *Huckleberry Finn,* Melville in *The Confidence-Man: His Masquerade,* and James, with typical indirection, in *The Wings of the Dove.* It has also seemed important to give considerable attention to smaller figures like the Southern humorists and to Bret Harte, for in regard to the confidence man they are significant writers of the period.

The fact that the confidence man intrigued our most important writers is one of the many reasons for studying him. Of course he is not, and I would not imply that he is, an intrinsically or exclusively "American" phenomenon. His qualities are too deeply rooted in a universal human nature and have been too often and too widely exploited for such a claim to be made. But the indigenous forms that he takes—Simon Suggs, Twain's "King" and "Duke"—are often held up as inimitably American characters. The reasons are largely the subject matter of this book, and yet I think it appropriate to make a few suggestions at the outset.

To begin with, it helps to consider the con man as a one-man enterprise, inspired just as much by the beauty of his scheme as by the need for aggrandizement. Viewed in this light, he represents an individualization of manifest destiny. He takes to heart the belief that a free man may be whatever he claims he is, may have whatever his skill can win, may feel at home in any man's house. Superior wit, skill in the use of resources, a nomadic and bachelor existence, adaptability, enthusiasm, and a continual desire to better one's condition—these are qualities associated with the type of character whom we think of as having "opened" our country. They are also qualities of the confidence man.

Leslie Fiedler has said that "geography in the United States is mythological,"[3] and perhaps a corollary of his meaning is that the individual who forages in this landscape may sense the archetypal qualities of his particular experience. When such a character turns his imagination upon himself and his struggles to survive, must not the result bear some resemblance to spontaneous myth-making? Such, at least, seems to have been the case with Bonner's Jim Beckwourth, who felt under "the obliga-

3. Leslie A. Fiedler, *The Return of the Vanishing American* (New York: Stein and Day, 1968), p. 16.

tion to lie gloriously"[4] and whose tall tales were the materials from which a "gorgeous folk-art resulted." The confidence games we shall look at have more in common with this richly imagined self-posturing, this American mythology, than they do with the cunning deceits of Iagos and Volpones. This study will follow the nineteenth-century American confidence man from his most artlessly artful days to his advent as a character with the broadest moral and philosophical suggestions for what is untrustworthy in his native land. His mercenary craft provides a rare meeting ground for Mark Twain and Henry James; his magnetic persuasions fascinate the realist in Howells and the romancer in Hawthorne and Melville. He is as irresistible as fool's gold, as hopeful as the promised land, as faithless as the gilded age.

Interesting as he is in himself, the confidence man is also worth studying for what he means to his creators. There are, it seems to me, important similarities between the "game" of confidence and the "art" of fiction. To begin with, both the "game" and the "art" have aesthetic form; both depend on an internally consistent representation of reality which sustains belief, even if it does not mirror actuality. Furthermore, since the "game" is generated by and predicated upon the known weaknesses of the victim, the confidence man's operations serve the turn of the satirist, the moralist, the critic of society. There is also a latent symbolism in the nature of any "con game," for it is a systematic and overt expression of a venerable theme—the confusion between appearance and reality. Indeed it even has an inherent philosophical bias; it suggests a comic-pessimistic view of the universe in which man is manipulated and victimized without gaining in stature. The fact that both the "game" and the "art" support an illusion by the control of rhetoric makes the relationship between the con-man character and his artist creator particularly sensitive and self-revealing.

For this is the century in which a writer like Hawthorne can feel guilt at the imposture of fiction as reality. Yet it is also the century in which the novel achieves stature as social critique. The confidence man lives by knowledge of the liabilities of

4. T. D. Bonner, *The Life and Adventures of James P. Beckwourth* (New York: Harper & Brothers, 1856), p. xxv.

human nature and of the particular foibles of a time and place. Thus he becomes especially useful to the writer of social commentary. Hawthorne, Melville, Mark Twain, and Howells all use him to get at his victims, to expose *them* to laughter, pity, or contempt. It is for us to see the folly to which these victims are blind. And to this extent, we, too, are in league with the confidence man.

PART I

Exploiting the Territory

CHAPTER ONE

From the East

For the child who comes upon the upper Hudson River in the pages of *The Last of the Mohicans*, it does not matter that the landscape is that of a Durand painting in a heavy gilt frame. For him the soft gurgle of the stream blends with the smothered laugh of the figure in the middle foreground. The crunch of a twig and the snap of a flintlock rifle are twin sounds that stab the ear and send a shiver to the heart. Under a "canopy of woods," beside a "glassy current" and enveloped in the "cooler vapours [that] rested in the atmosphere," emerges the figure of a man who the child knows must be lank and sinewy, must be clothed in supple deerskin, shod in trackless moccasins, caparisoned with a powderhorn, and weaponed with an infallible rifle that, upended, matches him in height. He must be these things because he is Natty Bumppo, the fictional embodiment of the backwoods hunter.

According to Timothy Flint, Cooper's hero is modeled on the character of Daniel Boone, and transforms that historic woodsman into a legendary figure.[1] He is an archetype for a list of reasons which may be headed by his "originality." Like Boone, he is a man who thinks and feels and performs in a "new" way—an American truly because he is, as Flint says, "a new man, the author and artificer of his own fortunes, and showing from the beginning rudiments of character, of which history has recorded no trace in his ancestors" (Flint, p. 12). Vulnerable as that statement is, it half explains the tenacity with

---

1. Timothy Flint, *The First White Man of the West; or, the Life and Exploits of Col. Dan'l Boone, The First Settler of Kentucky* (Cincinnati: Morgan & Co., 1850).

which Americans hold onto the image of the backwoods hunter. When he is gentled and ennobled by the influence of European romanticism, he becomes Natty Bumppo. And what is he like? He is a solitary, what Melville would call an "isolato," though without the metaphysical implications. If not alone, he is in company with other men who are the last of their tribe, like the stoical Chingachgook, whose minimal treasures are a "solitary eagle's plume" and an only son. Endowed with a legendary skill that makes him widely respected, this woodsman can read the print of a moccasin on dry rock and shoot a bullet through the opening of a distant water vessel. He is the embodiment of honesty, but he knows that survival can depend on deceit. Advising Major Heyward, whose notions of gallantry do not allow for subterfuge, he explains that " 'Whoever comes into the woods to deal with the natives, must use Indian fashions, if he would wish to prosper in his undertakings.' "[2] Thus, to get the better of a treacherous Indian guide, he tells the Major to "Talk openly to the miscreant, and seem to believe him the truest friend you have on 'arth.' "[3]

Survival is the daily business of life, not a long-range objective; to be solitary and to survive requires uncommon abilities, or what Leatherstocking would call "gifts." They are emphatically not those of a bookish intelligence, but rather those of an intuitive "mother-wit" aided by rugged experience. Among them is necessarily the ability to read human nature, especially "Indian natur'." Also, the hunter must be able to read the forest. When he sees only the tips of a deer's antlers, he must know where the two eyes will be. Several days' food may depend on it. When he sees the path of the migrating geese, he must infer all the points of the compass. His life will almost surely depend on it. In short, the backwoodsman must understand the ways of an often hostile environment and of the animal and human game he chases. Knowing only this, Cooper's Leatherstocking is driven westward by the encroachment of a civilization which would demand that he leave his gun by the door. In *The Pioneer* he says, for the seeming benefit of hack writers to come, " 'I'm

2. James Fenimore Cooper, *The Last of the Mohicans: A Narrative of 1757*, 3 vols. (London: John Miller, 1826), 1: 76.
3. Ibid.

weary of living in clearings, and where the hammer is sounding in my ears from sun-rise to sun-down.... I'm formed for the wilderness; and, if ye love me, let me go where my soul craves to be ag'in!' "[4]

But for the child who has once shivered in the deep forest where dark Indian limbs are lost in the swaying branches, there remains a sincere nostalgia which has nothing to do with Cooper's theories of social progress and westward movement, and which will remain even after the adult has laughed with Mark Twain at Cooper's literary offenses. Natty Bumppo has a skill commensurate with exigencies that are real, and because he has a knowledge commensurate with the life he is part of, our imagination is lenient toward this hunter whom Cady calls "the advance agent of American civilization, the knight of the wilderness."[5] Paradoxically, it is these archetypal characteristics—the skill in survival, superior quickness of hand, and richness of experience in the hunt—which make him the unexpectedly honorable ancestor of the asocial individualist, the canny manipulator of human weakness, and the poacher in the woods of society. Long before he might have witnessed such an indignity, however, he fades back into the varnished landscape; it is for us to see that certain traits compatible with his honesty carry a different suggestion when illustrated by the wilier hunters of the Kentucky frontier.

In contrast to Natty Bumppo, David Crockett is a man of the clearings as well as of the forest. He not only hears, but uses the hammer. He knows how to make cabins, hustings, or a banquet table. Sawdust clings to him as often as does the white frost or transparent dew of early morning expeditions into the forest. The legendary hunter and the backwoods politician come together in him and make a dubious hero. Lucy Hazard, in *The Frontier in American Literature*, presents an unsympathetic view of what she calls "the braggart bearhunter and petty politician." But her standards are not those of the popular mind. That mind takes its knowledge of Crockett al-

4. Cooper, *The Pioneers, or the Sources of the Susquehanna: A Descriptive Tale*, 2 vols. (New York: Charles Wiley, 1823): 2: 325–26.
5. Edwin Harrison Cady, *The Gentleman in America* (Syracuse: Syracuse University Press, 1949), p. 136.

most entirely from two laudatory accounts of a man dear to the people, and although the tales are of doubtful authenticity, their influence is a genuine phenomenon, and their "Davy Crockett" is effectively ours, too. It is worth a moment's attention to see how he helps us toward an understanding of the cagey Simon Suggs.

There is a persistent, though mild and generally ignored, incongruity in the character that emerges from the Crockett "biographies." It is perhaps nothing more than a shift of emphasis. Looking at the woodsman, clean-limbed, clear-eyed, and confident, we see him as he claimed to be, as trustworthy and as unbendingly true as the barrel of the gun he carried. One remembers the Crockett motto, "Be always sure you're right— THEN GO AHEAD!" which sounds so much like advice to a would-be marksman. And yet when the gun is raised to the shoulder, it fits there because of the accommodating curve in the wooden stock. Human nature, like the human body, at times requires a curve, an adjustment, a useful evasion which may be the better part of truth. And so it is with the engaging character of the homespun politician. He will circle around when the direct way is awkward or blocked by difficulties. One of Crockett's biographers says of him that he "was ever a mere sport for fortune . . . and in his wanderings appears to have been governed by the principle, that there was more beauty in a curve than in a straight line."[6] In other words, when you can't go ahead, go roundabout, with the obvious echo, "but be sure that you get there!" This may suggest the essential and even the American unity of character in this man of head-on integrity and side-stepping wisdom.

Like Natty Bumppo, Crockett is, in the straightforward sense, a hunter. He, too, is a man of legendary skill. However, the bear he hunts is as different from the sylvan deer as Crockett's sociable, lusty temperament is different from the ascetic dignity of Leatherstocking. The bear has a shaggy vest, is ponderous but light on its feet, blundering but coy, a scrambler, a runner, and even, at times, a walker. In short, he is more nearly a "human" adversary, as the manner of speaking about him indicates. Facing the bear, like challenging a man, is a test of personality as

6. David Crockett, *Sketches and Eccentricities of Col. David Crockett of West Tennessee* (New York: J. and J. Harper, 1833), p. 28.

well as of physical skill. According to the legends, even facial expression is important, as may be seen in the recurring theme of Crockett's paralyzing grin. The association between success in hunting and the power of presence, which is normally a social phenomenon, is, I think, instructive. There are some individuals whose innate ability to dominate and persuade (if not paralyze) the general run of people they meet allows them to live by other means than tilling the soil or shooting wild game. Crockett, though no confidence man, has qualities which would have made him an irresistible one.

For one thing, he, or his literary embodiment, to be more exact, is rhetorically aware of the romantic (literary) and democratic (political) "effects" to be gained by the backwoodsman who is both proud of his humble origin and anxious to rise above it. In praising the backwoodsman, Crockett uses the various voices which carry weight with audiences in the first half of the nineteenth century. In faultless Rousseau-ese he explains that, "to my mind, there is something refreshing in turning from the dissipation of a city to look upon a rural fête—from etiquette and rigid forms, to nature as it is."[7] This is stilted language, to be sure. One recalls and sympathizes with the anguish that William Carlos Williams felt over the artificial way in which Daniel Boone is made to tell of his union with the wilderness.[8] But on second thought, the posturing that Crockett seems to do here is in keeping with a characteristic quality all his own. He desires, whenever possible, to say that which will ingratiate him in the minds of his audience.

Occasionally he defends the backcountry in terms that have the ring of genuine feeling but also belong to a sentimental tradition. For example, returning from the Indian wars, he is greeted affectionately by his family, ". . . and though I was only a rough sort of a backwoodsman, they seemed mighty glad to see me, however little the quality folks might suppose it. For I do reckon we love as hard in the backwoods country, as any people in the whole creation."[9] In the same tradition he plays

7. Ibid., p. 48.
8. William Carlos Williams, *In the American Grain* (New York: New Directions, 1956), pp. 130–39.
9. David Crockett, *A Narrative of the Life of David Crockett, of the State of Tennessee* (Philadelphia: E. L. Carey and A. Hart, 1834), p. 123.

with the poor man's quaint preoccupation with high and low "birth." He notes the manner in which he was born, adding that "indeed, it might be inferred, from my present size and appearance, that I was pretty *well born*, though I have never yet attached myself to that numerous and worthy society."[10] It would be left to the confidence man to claim these associations when it pleased him to do so.

A corollary to the pride in humble beginnings is, as I have said, the urge to rise in the world, or at least to change locale. Although the language of the following passage suggests a Dickensian waif, it seems also to appropriate the glamour of the Ben Franklin tradition: "At length I resolved to leave him [my father] at all hazards.... For all other friends having failed, I determined then to throw myself on Providence, and see how that would use me."[11] Like Franklin, Crockett is writing his memoirs because Providence was unusually kind. Says Crockett toward the end of "his" book, "I want the world to understand my true history, and how I worked along to rise from a canebrake to my present station in life."[12] Crockett, like many of the confidence men we shall study, is a master of self-dramatization. He knows how to adopt a rhetoric of proven appeal. He can offer himself either as "one of the boys" or as a superior person—"the one who made good." But always he conveys an extraordinary sense of himself, his efficacy, his uniqueness. "Go where I will," he remarks at one point, "everybody seems anxious to get a peep at me." Despite his temporary setbacks and fears, the impression grows stronger that he is supremely self-assured. This, too, is true of the confidence man, who is after all primarily self-confident and self-knowing, whereas his victims are ready to grasp at the supports and flatteries offered them.

His rise in the world seems to accentuate the curves in Crockett's nature and to bring into relief the bends that were there from the beginning. As a boy he was adept at Tom Sawyerish escapades, climbing out windows, slipping down poles, surprising the family with dramatic returns after unexplained absences. On a more sophisticated level, he describes the courtship of his

10. Ibid., p. 17.
11. Ibid., p. 134.
12. Ibid., p. 172.

second wife: "I soon began to pay my respects to her in real good earnest; but I was as sly about it as a fox when he is going to rob a hen-roost." [13] In wooing the voters also he finds it necessary to skirt the main issue, for the simple reason that the formal workings of government are unknown to him. On one occasion, to disguise his lack of knowledge, he avoids all mention of the doubtful area and "keeps dark, going on the identical same plan that I now find is called '*non-commital.*'" [14] He finds that the voters respond as well to humorous anecdotes as they do to discussions of the judiciary. And he is cunning enough to end one speech with an invitation for all to join him in some liquid refreshment. This sort of diversionary tactic, which substitutes general knowledge of human nature for specific knowledge of the facts, pulls Simon Suggs and his descendants through many a tight place.

But his anecdotes of trickery are what put Crockett most directly within the scope of this study, and what show most clearly his delight in the devious methods of men who trap other men. There is, for example, the story about his own youthful prank of selling one coonskin to the same buyer over and over again, each time delivering it up for a trade in whiskey, repossessing it on the sly, and then offering it up as a new skin for barter. It is a tale that understandably caught Mark Twain's attention; he develops it into an anecdote of his own. Crockett also tells of Slim, the Yankee clock-peddler, jewelry salesman, and confidence man. In this story the backwoodsman drops openly into the role of psychological strategist. For, although everyone knows that to sell jewelry at its worth is to be merely a vendor, and that to try to sell it for more is to be a cheat, it is also generally understood that to sell it for apparent loss yet extravagant gain is to be a man of uncommon abilities. By way of example, Slim approaches the farmer's wife. She knows quite well that the jewelry is overpriced, even as she knows she is quite old enough to be the mother of the full-grown woman beside her. But Slim declares that he has been fooled: he thought the two women were sisters. He would never have thought—he still can't believe—and in fact the compliment of

13. Ibid., p. 127.
14. Ibid., pp. 139–40.

youth is not wholly undeserved; the old woman forgets her wisdom and buys as heedlessly as a young girl. Her husband is scarcely less willing to believe that his farm is, as Slim says, the best in the area. And so on.[15]

Slim is closely related to, if not reincarnated in, the Yankee of another Crockett anecdote. This time two foreigners meet him in the Mississippi Valley and ask for a display of that famous Yankee commodity, the "trick." At first declining, he at last promises to oblige them the following morning. But the next day the two foreigners discover that the trick has already been played. The Yankee has absconded with their clothes and luggage and is making his way downstream on a flatboat. Angered, they give chase in a fast skiff and overtake the Yankee. He greets them calmly and courteously. Did they like his demonstration of a Yankee trick? He thought it a good performance. He would help them load their goods back onto the skiff. Afterwards they would come aboard the flatboat and do him the honor of joining in a drink to the game. Mollified, they agree. They come aboard. The next thing they know, they are watching in amazement and despair as the Yankee jumps into the laden skiff and disappears upstream and away.[16]

In each of these episodes there is a structure with an aesthetic unity which perhaps only the victims fail to appreciate. In fact the trick as anecdote suggests the closeness between the trickster and the storyteller in their appreciation of form and style. Both plan the "build-up," engineer the reversals, time the climax, and take pleasure in capping their work with a "clincher." Also, Crockett as raconteur shows his delight in the vagaries of human

15. Slim's relationship to Sam Slick, the Clockmaker, will be evident to anyone who has met the confidence man created by Thomas Chandler Haliburton. Although strictly speaking Slim is not within the scope of an American study, his technique of "soft sawder" (flattery) and "human natur" (appeal to vanity and love of luxury) is part of the heritage of the American confidence man.

16. There is an interesting parallel to this story to be found among the Indian tales collected in Mody C. Boatright's *The Sky Is My Tipi*. The white man begs the clever Coyote for a demonstration of one of his famous tricks. Coyote refuses at first, but at last agrees to get his "medicine" if the white man will give him his horse to ride home for it. Before the end of the story, Coyote has taken all that the white man has, and is able to jeer at him for having been thoroughly fleeced.

nature. The stories are in a sense humorous forms of village satire, with the simple vanities of the farmer or the foolish curiosity of the foreigner as the target. But it also seems to be true that Crockett as bear-hunter, Indian-fighter, and electioneer takes natural interest in a tale of difficulties met and overcome by superior intelligence. Crockett, after all, knows the value of being able to hold a listener and to direct other people's imaginations in prearranged ways. That he is not in fact a confidence man is a tribute to the reality of those virtues emphasized in the legends, the children's books, and the reincarnations on television. That he proudly possesses so many attributes of the insinuator is a measure of the folk interest, the frontier reputation, and perhaps even the Americanism of the confidence man.

In judging the wider significance of the confidence man, however, one must begin with the development of that character in the hands of the Southern humorists. For them he becomes something more complex than the canny salesman of Yankee tradition and something less monumental than the cunning backwoodsman. He begins, quite unpretentiously, as a practical joker who understands human nature well enough to manipulate its stock behavior patterns for his own amusement.

Ned Brace is a "Native Georgian" in Augustus B. Longstreet's humorous book, *Georgia Scenes, Characters, Incidents, &c. in the First Half Century of the Republic* (1835). Thus closely associated with a particular time, region, and population, he is nevertheless entirely an individual, conscious of abilities that distinguish him from the generality of those he encounters. The infallible eyesight and the mastery of weapons we have seen associated with the hunters of animal game are here transformed into the infallible insight possessed by the student of men and the mastery of tone, gesture, and suggestion possessed by the gifted actor. The confidence man in his fullest development, it should be remembered, is both the contriver and the performer of his own small comedies. Even in his milder form as the practical joker like Ned Brace, his skill is his intelligence and his weapon is himself or the characters he can assume. In the sketch called "The Character of a Native Georgian," he and the narrator are traveling and arrive at an inn where they are total strangers to all present. The advent into new territory is always an opportunity for defining oneself anew and on one's own terms. Ned decides to take advantage of this fact to arrange an elaborate joke. Two stages in this game deserve special attention because they are classical examples of a tension between the straight and the curved, between, as we now say colloquially, the "straight man" and the comic man.

Inside the tavern Ned is approaching, the gathering of guests around the fire is pleasantly animated and only briefly disturbed by the entry of Ned's friend, the narrator, who has traveled ahead. After stating his name to the barkeeper, he joins the group to which he has been thus summarily introduced. He is admitted easily and matter-of-factly. A few moments later Ned arrives and, according to custom, is asked his name. Ned delays. At last he complies with obvious reluctance by offering a slip of paper with an unintelligible scrawl written on it. Taking a place in the group, he remains so silent that the general conversation is lamed and finally paralyzed. Quite unexpectedly, Ned removes himself and leaves the others to a lively assault on the problem of his identity and character. The slip of paper is examined while he is thought to be out of the room, and the mortification is general when he suddenly reappears and coldly asks to have it returned. The barkeeper extends his hand and the paper. Ned delays. He does not accept it until the barkeeper has become thoroughly nonplussed. Thus by repeatedly disrupting the normal relationship between expectation and result, he compels his victims to grant him his own terms.

And these terms require the acceptance of regulated amounts of absurdity. At dinner the guests reassemble around the hostess's table. Not knowing what to expect from the mysterious stranger, they are able to accept anything. The hostess asks whether he would like tea or coffee. He politely explains that it is his custom to take both at once. Offered various breads, rolls, and muffins, he helps himself to samples of each and proceeds to mince and mash them into a paste. This he molds and smooths with his knife, as carefully as a child would trim a mudpie. The others are stunned but refrain from comment. And of course it is for the sake of his own comic enjoyment of their awed seriousness that Ned endures the torture of eating his mangled food. As before he delayed and withheld beyond all expectation, he now plunges and gathers in, confusing everyone by his energy as before he did by his lethargy. His rule is to break the rule.

There are of course many more turns to be taken before the joke is played out. Ned wins the sympathy of the landlady by pretending to be sensitively aware of his abnormality. He greets entire strangers as old friends and generally seizes every opportunity to confound and disorient the people around him. It is true that his schemes are for amusement rather than profit, but this extenuation does not change the fact that there are many similarities between Ned Brace and the true confidence man. Aesthetically, there is the shared delight in sustaining a self-imposed character or caricature. We know that Ned "could assume any character which his humour required him to personate, and he could sustain it to perfection. His knowledge of the character of others seemed to be intuitive." [17] In social terms, there is the same often-repeated pattern of the outsider arriving, working out his game, and then disappearing again. Morally, too, there is a similarity. Both lack concern for the pain or discomfort incidentally or directly caused to their victims. Both practice a kind of extortion, the toll being paid in one case by money, in the other by chagrin. If one remembers Mark Twain's suffering as the victim of various practical jokes, it is not too much to say that both games may be cruel. Finally, Ned Brace and the confidence man are both useful as instruments of social criticism. Longstreet himself tells us that "the beau in the presence of his mistress, the fop, the pedant, the purse-proud, the over-fastidious and sensitive, were Ned's favorite game." [18] These terms, which come from eighteenth-century English satire and comedy, are really of little significance to the story except to indicate the author's satirical impulse. What Ned Brace really shows us is the special interrelatedness of the joke, the exhibition, and the game—a pattern suggestive of the origins of the American confidence man. It is significant, too, that Ned Brace works

17. Augustus B. Longstreet, *Georgia Scenes, Characters, Incidents, &c, in the First Half Century of the Republic,* 2nd ed. (New York: Harper & Brothers, 1840), pp. 32–33.
18. Ibid., p. 32.

by playing upon the human capacity to become interested in novel or exaggerated conditions of life. Crockett, we may recall, once compared himself to an exhibit in a crowd-drawing sideshow. The ability to make oneself an object of interest particularly suited to the capacity for naive wonder—this, combined with the actor's delight in impersonation—is a further characteristic of such widely different con men as Mark Twain's King and Melville's Cosmopolitan.

For our purposes, Ned Brace, the practical joker, is succeeded briefly and partially by John Robb's hero in the first part of *Streaks of Squatter Life* (1843). John Earl is an itinerant adventurer, accomplished role-player, versatile orator, jack-of-all-trades, and brilliant opportunist. Above all he is a master of ingratiation, with great benefit to his financial standing. The Franklin motif of rising in the world is very important in the history of John Robb's traveling typographer. So, too, is the sentimental tradition of chivalry to widows and of tearful reunions. Yet he interests us because he does not take himself or his future too seriously, because he is a cheerful disciple of luck and a believer in the short-term issue. He is "intelligent, reckless, witty, improvident, competent, and unsteady—"[19] and like others after him, he conceives of the West as "that mighty corn field—that region of pork and plenty—land of the migrating sucker—haven of hope, and country of adventure...."[20] There is no advocate of America's bounty like the confidence man who preys upon its "sucker" population.

In Robb's book there is also a brief sketch entitled " 'Doing' a Landlord." Tom is the character who is in need of money. As it happens, he is also "a genius, whose ideas of life [are] on such a magnificent scale that they [outrun] his interest, capital and all."[21] He is sitting disconsolately on the front porch of a hotel where his credit has been suspended. Enter, to him, a human representative of "pork and plenty." The newly arrived gentleman, who under the circumstances may very well have been

---

19. John S. Robb, *Streaks of Squatter Life, and Far-West Scenes* (Gainesville, Fla.: Scholars' Facsimiles and Reprints, 1962), p. 11.

20. Ibid., p. 13.

21. Ibid., p. 21.

corpulent, ascends the stairs and approaches in Tom's direction. After a quick and reassuring inspection of his own coat, Tom accosts the gentleman: " 'Excuse me, sir, but you look so like an old friend of mine, J. B.' "[22] It is a Ned Brace joke, but this time with a financial incentive. Tom makes himself so engaging that he is invited inside the hotel and takes a table with the gentleman. At once a waiter is sent to collect the money due from Tom, but receives instead an indignant frown. How outrageous, Tom exclaims to his new friend, to be dunned like this when the waiter, and for that matter, the landlord must know very well that he is only temporarily out of funds until his property arrives in a trunk. Eager to be helpful, the representative of "pork and plenty" lends Tom a one-thousand-dollar bill. The bill is almost immediately returned, but not until the sight of it restores Tom's credit at the hotel, and not before the news of it extends his credit all over town. As a coup it is surpassed only by Twain's escapade in *The Million Dollar Banknote*, in which a very similar and perhaps even borrowed ploy is used. For a period of six months Tom lives off this misplaced confidence in the expected arrival of a large trunk. In time the trunk is received, and before it is discovered to be full of stones, Tom has made a strategic escape from that part of the country. Not even Simon Suggs could have done more with the same material. And yet, no doubt, he would have done it with greater style.

Long of nose, long of coat, and rather short of trousers and of honesty, Simon Suggs is initially presented to us as a man who might one day be called upon to represent us in the legislature. *Some Adventures of Captain Simon Suggs* (1845), ostensibly a "campaign biography" in the tradition of the Crockett tales, is introduced with all the officiousness of the genteel biographer, and all the slyness of the tongue-in-cheek humorist. Hooper tells us that "our friend is about fifty years old, and seems to indurate as he advances in years."[23] Except for the tone, this line might pass for a description of Bumppo in later life, when "every

22. Ibid., p. 162.
23. Johnson Jones Hooper, *Some Adventures of Captain Simon Suggs* (Philadelphia: H. C. Baird, 1850), p. 11. Future page references given in text.

nerve and muscle appeared strung and indurated by unremitted exposure and toil."[24] Our friend, as Hooper so engagingly calls him, also toils, in his way, although he tends to expose others rather than himself. He, too, is the master of unusual skills. He is "a miracle of shrewdness. He possesses, in an eminent degree, that tact which enables a man to detect the *soft spots* in his fellow" (p. 12). This is an ability not so different from that "gift" which enables a man to take his aim and direct his fire at the vital organs of the deer, the bear, and the Indian. Only in one instance the keen eye is a steady one, while in the other it is notoriously shifty. Or, again, we learn that our candidate "has a quick, ready wit, which has extricated him from many an unpleasant predicament, and which makes him whenever he chooses to be so—and that is always—very companionable" (pp. 12–13). As a result, he can "assimilate himself to whatever company he may fall in with." The frontier life has always put a premium on surefootedness and agility, whether of mind or body, and on the resourcefulness by which one recognizes the useful and either appropriates it or adapts easily to it. For Leatherstocking, and indeed for Daniel Boone as William Carlos Williams sees him, this adaptation is measured by an approximation to the Indian way of life; for Crockett, adaptation includes the politician's readiness to adjust to the humor of the crowd; for Suggs, adaptation is altogether a function of the particular moment and its special conditions. That tendency to indurate, to harden, which Hooper describes, is surely a toughening of the sinews of self-preservation, which precludes any "soft spots" in Simon Suggs. Ignoble as he appears in comparison with the masters of the long rifle, he is, after all, a descendant of theirs and a candidate for our admiration, if not for our vote. He offers to represent us. We, in turn, must deal with the cultural and literary fact that he is successful. He prevails even though "his whole ethical system lies snugly in his favorite aphorism—IT IS GOOD TO BE SHIFTY IN A NEW COUNTRY—which means that it is right and proper that one should live as merrily and comfortably as possible at the expense of others" (p. 12). And here we may remember with a smile the words of Captain Farrago to his unprincipled servant: "You have nothing but your character,

24. Cooper, *The Last of the Mohicans*, p. 47.

Teague, in a new country to depend upon."[25] The world of *Modern Chivalry* is of the eighteenth century, but one reads about it with the feeling that it awaits Simon Suggs for the full effect of its ironies to be felt.

Suggs's first impetus toward a life of crime is the pleasure he takes in cheating his slave at cards; the second is his desire to avoid punishment for playing with cards at all. Simon first encounters authority in the form of the narrow ethic and narrower mind of his father, a "hard-shell" Baptist to whom cards are anathema, and the first weapon he finds is the worldly vanity of that same Baptist mind. But at the moment Simon and Ben are deep in their clandestine game of cards. Simon is calmly cheating his companion, apparently as much from a sense of mastery as for the money he is able to win. They are interrupted by the appearance of the man who represents doom to both of them, and he comes bearing a mulberry branch that is stripped and limber and tingling to look upon. A whipping seems as inevitable as fate, but Simon does not accept a world-order that cannot be tampered with by the ingenuity of the people directly concerned. Therefore, he adroitly begins to suggest that the mysteries of gaming are known only to those who, like their neighbor Bob Smith, have seen the world—or at least Augusta. Piqued at this disregard for his own travels, the father becomes interested against his will. Eventually he agrees to let Simon demonstrate a card trick that seems impossible. Simon has already arranged that if he himself fails, he will "give" to his father all the money he has; if he is successful, his father will "give" him the family horse and a chance to leave home. To the old man, this arrangement of contingent gifts bears no relation to the sin of gambling. As for Simon, he is ready to take his winnings under whatever name is acceptable to the loser. He performs his trick and leaves his father believing helplessly that predestination has had a hand in the business somewhere, and that it was all fixed beforehand. Delightedly Simon plays with the word, admitting that, indeed, the cards *were* "fixed." And so his first triumph becomes not only an escape from punish-

25. Hugh Henry Brackenridge, *Modern Chivalry: Containing the Adventures of Captain John Farrago and Teague O'Regan, His Servant*, ed. Lewis Leary (New Haven: College and University Press, 1965), p. 40.

ment, not only a victory of intelligence, but also a license to begin life anew on his own account. Like more respectable knights errant, he has a horse to carry him and a faith to guide him. But his horse is property to be capitalized on, and his faith is in the providence of wit.

His various escapades are too numerous to be described in full, but several achieve a classic stature which must be noted here. The first has to do with the circumstances that make Suggs the Captain of the Tallapoosa Volunteers. The scene, as it often is on the backwoods stage, is an isolated cabin under the threat of attack by hostile Indians. Suggs alone, by virtue of the con man's greatest advantage—superior information—knows that the threat has no basis in fact, and that there is absolutely no danger. Thus he is in the unique position of being at ease in the midst of a terrified group of people. Their cowardice and naive impressionability become the lever of his advantage, as his father's vanity and greed had been before. Suggs aptly proposes the formation of a volunteer force and easily puts himself in charge of it. Thereafter he maintains his importance by keeping the fears aroused and by employing the rhetoric of stage battles and wooden-sword flourishes. The whole is, of course, a burlesque. A comic figure, a stout old woman who crosses the picket lines to get a bit of tobacco for her pipe, is given a farcical court martial by a "drum-head" court. The formalities of this procedure are invented by Suggs on the spot. So is an improvised army uniform. Sternly impressive, he subjects the woman to agonizing terrors by pretending to see her case as a serious violation of military discipline during wartime. Having threatened her with death, he pretends to relent and to be moved by chivalrous pity to demand only the payment of a fine. Allowing a tear to form in his eye, he declares, " 'I never *could* bar to see a woman suffer! it strikes me right *here*!' and the Captain placed his hand upon his breast in a most impressive manner" (p. 109). The combination of sentimentality and thespian gesture is broadly comic to the reader and to Suggs. To the desperate Mrs. Haycock, on trial for her life, it is infinitely gracious. To anyone who takes the events too literally, it is also implacably cruel, thus to torture the defenseless and then to rob them in the name of clemency. But surely the art of the storyteller, Hooper, combines with the art of the con man, Suggs, to leave us with the impression that the whole affair is *not* to be taken too literally. It has been staged for the sake of the laugh. The moral seems to be that, if the world is a stage, then it behooves one to star in one's own play.

With Mark Twain's help, the camp-meeting episode has become perhaps the most famous of the Suggs adventures. It begins with a description of the audience: "Men and women rolled about on the ground, or lay sobbing or shouting in promiscuous heaps" (p. 119). The creator of this effect is the minister who is preaching to them, providing the yeast for their religious ecstasies as Suggs had done for the terrors of his volunteers. Very naturally, Suggs regards the preacher as a rival. "He [views] the whole affair as a grand deception—a sort of 'opposition line' running against his own, and [looks] on with a sort of professional jealousy" (p. 122). As though in answer to a challenge, he rises and begins to tell of his own experiences with sin, knowing exactly what his audience expects and desires to hear. As no performance is complete without its reward in cash, Suggs appeals to the congregation for money "to found a church in his own neighborhood" (p. 130). The wealthy are enjoined to give first, and then Simon deftly implies that those who give less are no doubt constrained by their poverty to do so, and thus he "[excites] the pride of purse of the congregation" (p. 131). No doubt, too, it is the preacher's turn to feel professional jealousy, for it is not outside the realm of possibility that he has been bettered at his own game. After all, there is very little difference in the religious quality of the experience Suggs offers the audience, unless indeed it be more cathartic to both the spirit and the purse. The highly stereotyped vocabulary of the primitive evangelist is easily imitated, easily parodied, and is almost a staple of frontier humor. Certainly it reaches comic heights both here and in the camp-meeting harangue of the King in *Huckleberry Finn*. At least one critic, Bernard DeVoto, finds the Hooper original greater than the Twain adaptation, because it avoids pure buffoonery and is therefore better as satire while being equally effective as humor.[26]

26. Bernard DeVoto, *Mark Twain's America and Mark Twain at Work* (Boston: Houghton Mifflin Company, 1967), p. 255.

None of the professions are outside Simon's range, provided that they manifest themselves in a distinctive rhetoric and involve a broad contact with the population. From impromptu evangelist, he becomes a *de facto* legislator, simply because he happens to be riding in a train with a man who suspects him of actually being a congressman. Shifting immediately into the role, Simon yet maintains an air of wishing to keep his importance a secret. At the same time he artfully forgets himself in judicious slips of the tongue that confirm his "real" identity as a government official. It soon becomes apparent that his companion is a candidate for a bank directorship, and that his chances of success depend on his favor with the government. Believing that Suggs can be of use to him, he describes his hopes and then ostentatiously denounces those who, in his position, would stoop to bribing a congressman. Suggs agrees. He then drops his coy incognito, admits that he is a congressman, and tells his own story of righteousness unrewarded. It seems no one would advance him traveling expenses, despite the excellent security of his future wages as an elected representative. Deeply grieved, he had offered to walk the distance that would remain when his railway fare gave out. The banker, who is of course eager to flatter him, comments on Suggs's gesture in the following terms: " 'Yes, sir, it was a sublime moral spectacle, worthy of comparison with any recorded specimens of Roman or Spartan magnanimity, sir' " (p. 45). It is the sort of diction and the sort of allusion that is inseparable from the political oratory of the period. Suggs admits the justice of the tribute, and allows the banker to advance him the money his less feeling constituents had refused him. The Captain's behavior after he has pocketed the cash is fine proof of the fact that his love of the game is at least as great as his love of the money. When the banker says that he hopes the "congressman" is as honest as he appears, Suggs cannot resist a final performance: " 'Look me in the eye!' replied the Captain with an almost tragic air. The candidate looked steadily, for two seconds, in Simon's tearful eye. 'You see honesty thar—don't you?' 'I do! I do!' said the candidate with emotion" (p. 50).

It is the kind of outrageous sentimentality he offered to the woman he was pretending to court-martial. Here, of course, the irony revolves around the fact that the candidate actually believes he has bribed a congressman. So long as we are not asked for anything deeper than an intellectual appreciation of the banker's hypocrisy and Simon's adroit use of it, the scene remains purely and refreshingly comic. In the Hooper stories there is no Huck Finn for whom the "soul butter" turns rancid until it sickens the heart.

Perhaps the most fully developed game played by Suggs involves his impersonation of General Thomas Witherspoon, a rich Kentucky hog-drover. As before, a chance hint gives him the cue. In a gaming salon he hears the eminent person mentioned, and learns that the man's nephew is in the room. For Simon it is a routine matter to identify himself as General Witherspoon and to strengthen his claim by pretending to doubt the authenticity of the nephew. When Suggs is at last prevailed upon to accept the young man as a bona fide relative, "the tears rolled down his face, as naturally as if they had been called forth by real emotion, instead of being pumped up mechanically to give effect to the scene" (p. 62). The choice of the mechanistic image and the terms "scene" and "effect" are common also in Mark Twain's writings about confidence men, with implications that will be considered later on in this study. For now, let it suffice to say that again the pattern is that of wit taking advantage of human nature. Letting it be known that he would condescend to borrow money only from certain, select people, he makes everyone in the room think "how difficult and desirable a thing it would be, to lend money to General Thomas Witherspoon, the rich hog drover" (p. 61). This, to describe it by its more famous analogue, is the fence-white-washing technique used so successfully by Tom Sawyer. Both the old con man and the quick-witted boy know that people will vie with each other to do what it seems a privilege to do, however undesirable the act in itself may be.

Suggs, then, is a man supremely confident in himself and supremely able to create confidence in others. He is also squarely in the tradition of the anti-intellectual backwoodsman who lives by natural cunning, skill in the use of his weapons, and the knack of profiting by his experience. On one occasion Simon passes a display of law books in a window, only to comment,

" 'Well, mother-wit kin beat book-larning, at *any* game! . . . Human natur' and the human family is *my* books' " (p. 53). With this equipment he is an artificer in the constructive sense, for he builds each time a structure of claims and assurances, identities and ideas which, like any other artist, he makes his audience temporarily accept. We should note that creating something out of nothing is the morally acceptable version of getting something for nothing, and it is in fact embedded in the tradition of American experience, whether it be the creation of towns out of the wilderness or of a "fortune from scratch." The very word most often applied to Suggs, "shifty," has a history in which admirable and reprehensible qualities are blended. "Shift" originally meant a share, portion, or division of property. Eventually it came to mean "an expedient, an ingenious device for effecting some purpose" (*Oxford English Dictionary*). The meanings associated with resourcefulness and manner of livelihood were finally subsumed under the morally neutral terms of "an expedient necessitated by stress of circumstances; a forced measure." Complementing this use, however, is the clearly pejorative meaning of "a fraudulent or evasive device, a stratagem; a piece of sophistry, an evasion, subterfuge." Simon is a master of all of these, and yet he is also a hero of ingenuity and acumen, who is always equal to the very real stress of circumstance, loosely interpreted as the need for money. Because he never fully apprehends the consequences of his actions, and, by grace of his mobility, is never forced to deal with these consequences, his unromantic escapades are set in a strangely romantic context of unlimited freedom, invincible talent, and between-chapter escapes into a land where no one seems able to follow him. It is also, as I have stressed, a context from which the heart is missing. The history of Suggs is in almost classic terms a comic odyssey.

In the tradition of Southern humor, Suggs is followed by Joseph Baldwin's Simon Suggs, Jr., and also by his Ovid Bolus, the artistic liar. The first of these is a lawyer whose chicanery is venal without being greatly interesting, except as a tribute to the name and fame of Hooper's creation. But Bolus is a development of one aspect of the Suggs character which becomes important to the subsequent literature of the lie. His skill deserves a complete account:

Bolus was a natural liar, just as some horses are natural pacers, and some dogs natural setters. What he did in that walk, was from the irresistible promptings of instinct, and a disinterested love of art ... he did not labor a lie; he lied with a relish; he lied with a coming appetite, growing with what it fed on: he lied from the delight of invention and the charm of fictitious narrative. It is true he applied his art to the practical purposes of life; but in so far did he glory the more in it; just as an ingenious machinest rejoices that his invention, while it has honored science, has also supplied a common want.

In the mock-heroic vein, Baldwin continues:

Bolus's lying came from his greatness of soul and his comprehensiveness of mind. The truth was too small for the fervor of his genius. Besides, great as was his memory—for he even remembered the outlines of his chief lies—his invention was still larger. He had a great contempt for history and historians. ... He had long ceased to distinguish between the impressions made upon his mind by what came *from* it, and what came *to* it: all ideas were facts to him. ... He did not confine himself to mere lingual lying: ... He acted lies as well. Sometimes his very silence was a lie.[27]

"All ideas were facts to him." This might be the epitaph for many of the confidence men who will appear in this study. In a sense it is true that in a land where the facts of flora, fauna, geography, and meteorology were often incredible, the merely possible, even the merely improbable, often kept company with the truly factual. We are a gullible race. And this consideration leads us to recall that from the beginning in America there has been a concern with the difference between the innocence that preserves and the experience that corrupts. But these moral judgments have operated on one level only. For example, they are implicit in the theology of the New Englanders, and they inform the highly complex relationships in Henry James's novels. But on the folk level and in the backwoods, there is a corollary distinction between the naiveté that loses and the cunning that gains. In speaking of the Tennessee mountaineers in Miss Murfree's stories, Lucy L. Hazard refers to "the pathetic simplicity which ... facilitates their fleecing by those shrewder than themselves."[28] Here, of course, the moral judgment has reversed itself.

27. Joseph G. Baldwin, *The Flush Times of Alabama and Mississippi: A Series of Sketches* (New York: D. Appleton and Co., 1853), pp. 3–6.
28. Lucy L. Hazard, *The Frontier in American Literature* (New York: Barnes & Noble, 1941), p. 81.

It is believed that the foolish man condemns himself and deserves his defeat. There is no sympathy for him; only applause for the winner. The difference between the "greenhorn" and the veteran is yet another version of this distinction which favors the knowledgeable and the acclimated over the unprepared and the unfit. It is from this underside view of the matter that the confidence man emerges as an "original" of merit, a figure of strength, and a representative of that in us which would be cynically aware, yet tolerantly amused, admittedly self-centered, yet aesthetically detached, living by the facts of life, yet mastering them by fiction.

CHAPTER TWO

To the West

The backwoods pioneer moved westward in the path of Daniel Boone, playing a game of encounters with the Indian and sometimes losing a son to the hatchet. Taking even greater risks, the mountaineer penetrated the wilderness as a fur-trapper. Then, at last, came '49. The promised land was not Kentucky then, but California. And into the very fabric of the hopes and activities of the Gold Rush was woven the promise of the confidence game, the bet on "a sure thing."

The odds in favor of wealth tempted men of all kinds to cross the great gulf of land between the old frontier (now part of the "East") and the new frontier of the West. They followed such trapper-scouts as Jim Bridgers, Kit Carson, and the semifabulous Jim Beckwourth. A far different man was Beckwourth—adventure-bitten, lie-spinning, gore-loving "squaw man"—from the virtuous and dignified Boone. It is as though the greatly enlarged scale of the West could distend the imagination with the stuff of legend which experience tended rather to credit than to deny. Indeed, from the very beginning the conditions surrounding such men as Beckwourth bred a confusion of fact and fiction, interweaving them so subtly that accounts of our heroic period can never be entirely separated from a many-stranded myth.

Typical, perhaps, of the kind of tale that is hard to believe and yet easy to accept is the story of how the uncouth Jim Beckwourth himself brought into the new country a child destined to know and encourage the man who would put the gamble of the West into romantic literature.[1] This part of the legend of

1. The following account of the arrival of Ina Coolbrith is drawn from

the mountain man tells of his aiding a beleaguered wagon train and guiding it safely through his own pass in the Rockies. On his saddlebow he carried a very young girl who seems to have believed him every inch the hero he thought he was. And he was not her first experience with semilegendary men. Born Josephine D. Smith, she was a niece of the Mormon prophet, Joseph Smith. She survived the persecution of this religious group and had an adventurous career which took her to the "jumping-off place" at St. Louis and to the pueblo of Los Angeles. During these years she lived through many lives and was briefly married in one of them. Finally she emerged in San Francisco, taking on yet another role as a member of a literary circle. She became the virginal poetess of the Golden Gate, known as Ina Coolbrith, friend and inspiration of Charles Warren Stoddard, Prentice Mulford, Joaquin Miller, Francis Brett Harte, and Samuel Clemens. Once again she was on the saddlebow of a legend.

Contrast with her, if you will, another and older literary lady from the East, a quiet and gracious schoolteacher who lived in San Francisco and encouraged the first writing efforts of Charles Warren Stoddard.[2] Her first years in California were during the early Gold Rush. At that time she was quite prosaically married to a physician who took her with him into the mining camps and set her to housekeeping with oilcloth for table linen. There she encountered many picturesque individuals, one of whom may actually have been Jim Beckwourth. But he seems to have been no more than a curiosity to her; she remains resolutely straightforward. For one thing, there was no mystery about her origins; from the canyons and gulches of the new country in 1851–52 she wrote letters to the chintz parlors of her sister in New England, keeping a girlish promise to record accurately and fully the life of the mining camps. She, too, chose another name, but only for the transparent and limited purposes of a literary pseudonym. The letters of "Dame Shirley" were published serially in the *Pioneer* during 1854–55, and give what many (including Stoddard) consider the most vivid picture of the milieu

---

Franklin Walker, *San Francisco's Literary Frontier* (New York: Alfred A. Knopf, 1939), pp. 57–64.

2. Charles Warren Stoddard, *In the Footprints of the Padres* (San Francisco: A. M. Robertson, 1902), p. 92.

that Bret Harte later romanticized. The letters have a spritely and affectionate tone that can turn severe but objective when dealing with the more brutal facts of camp life. Altogether, with her good sense, spirit of adventure, and delight in natural beauty —her ability to improvise a home-in-the-rough and to love the experience—this decorous and chatty girl is an amazingly satisfactory historian for a turbulent and almost entirely masculine enterprise.

And here, in these ladylike epistles, we may pick up the trail of the confidence man. In an interesting way, it is really a false trail. As we look among the scores of miners, American and foreign, who inhabit Shirley's Rich Bar and Indian Bar, we come upon a storekeeper who is known as "Yank." In his former Eastern life he was a Yankee peddler, and with that strange, national twist of ideals that Mrs. Trollope had noted in her description of the Yankee, he insists on claiming for his generous and honest nature the repute and "merit" of being " 'cute and smart." Says Shirley, "[He] takes me largely into his confidence, as to the various ways he has of *doing* green miners. All the merest delusion on his part, you understand—."[3] It is an amusing instance of the good man wanting to seem worse than he is, but it shows how easy it is to translate the superior wit of the con man into the national virtue of acumen—and vice versa. Shirley obviously considers "Yank" as more of a curiosity than a threat to the miners, green or veteran, and she saves her indignation on this score for the professional gambler: "If a fortunate or an unfortunate (which shall I call him?) *does* happen to make a 'big strike,' he is almost sure to fall into the hands of the professed gamblers, who soon relieve him of all care of it. . . . But enough of these best-beloved of Beelzebub, so infinitely worse than the robber or murderer. . . ."[4] She does, however, recognize that the gambler is a prototypical figure on the Western frontier: ". . . the whole mining system in California is one great gambling, or better, perhaps—lottery transaction. It is impossible to tell whether a 'claim' will prove valuable or not."[5]

3. Louise Amelia K. Clappe [Dame Shirley], *The Shirley Letters from the California Mines, 1851–52* (New York: Alfred A. Knopf, 1949), p. 79.
4. Ibid., p. 137.
5. Ibid., pp. 50–51.

Attitudes toward the slick gambler illustrate as well as anything the Western tension between fact and fiction—between
the literal experience of the camp as recorded by a lively but
conservative housewife, and the romantic version of that experience as recreated by the bohemian literati. Shirley saw the
gambler as perhaps he was, a man of greasy cards and greasier
morals; Bret Harte saw him as a romantic hero who lives by
and conquers through the taking of chances. Harte's gambler
incarnates the Western version of the hunter ideal—the invincible man of superior wit, legendary skill, and power of personality. He is the dominant character, but there are others who
resemble him, and among the whole catalogue there is more than
one confidence man. Let us take Harte on his own terms for a
moment, and examine the West that he made.

For all its democracy his California has its castes, just as surely
as does Cable's Louisiana. And here the gambler has a rank
of his own. He does not have the social prestige of the visiting
English baronet, nor does he wield the power of the Eastern
financier or the San Francisco banker. These men, when they
do appear, often play the role of the *deus ex machina*—or perhaps even the devil out of the machine. In any case, they may
represent at least temporarily the "ace high" which carries all
before it. But the true kings in Bret Harte's country are the
nouveaux riches and the men of character and persistence who
might, at any turn of the spade, find fortune and prestige as did
Royal Thatcher. One recalls that Mr. Thatcher (in *The Story
of a Mine*) took as his queen a Mexican girl whose uncle was as
good as a forger and worse than a thief. Yet the sentimental tradition of Western chivalry assumed that there was a lady somewhere in every woman, and that therefore any woman might
become a queen. In moral terms this allowed for a universal payment of deference and courtesy, and for the pathetic irony,
reminiscent of old puns on "quaen," in the title of the "Duchess"
of Poker Flat. In literary terms such a view allowed Harte to
create a series of heroines with initial spices of the peculiar in
dress, manner, age, or situation, all of which could resolve at
last into a sugared simulacrum of the loving little woman. Every-
man is potentially a king, Everywoman a queen.

But the Jacks are wild, they are independent, they are eccentric. Each in his respective domain exercises absolute rule by the divine right of an irresistible personality. Nowhere is Harte more aristocratic than in postulating only one Yuba Bill, sovereign of the stagecoach, only one John Oakhurst, lord of the poker table, and only one Jack Hamlin, prince of all hearts. It is he of whom Gabriel Conroy's sister says, "She thought she had never known a more engaging person than this Knave of Clubs."[6] The quality of the exceptional in the two gamblers is emphasized by the fact that in a loosely constructed and porous society they are nevertheless outcasts; in a lawless and tolerant society they are nonetheless outlaws. Oakhurst becomes a literal outcast-outlaw in the story which ends in his death. Hamlin is more flexible and yet perhaps more fatalistic; he endures as a kind of vagabond troubadour caroling through the woods, disreputable in the abstract, lovable in the particular. Unlike Suggs but like a new kind of confidence man to come, he is a scamp with a "Raphael face." With a few notable exceptions he remains in our minds longer than the average member of the rest of the pack, the schoolmasters, editors, lawyers, doctors, preachers, farmers, miners, tramps, prostitutes, Indians, and Chinese. These are the main characters of Harte's West, and he shuffled and reshuffled them as long as he lived.

Luck, which tends to corrupt a wage-earning ethic, was a more than ordinarily important factor in the lives of these characters. Even where merit existed, labor and reward were so unevenly matched that living by the sweat of one's brow was in effect living by the spin of a roulette wheel. In *Three Partners* Demorest defends Jack Hamlin's occupation by saying, " 'I can't say that I see much difference in gambling by putting money into a hole in the ground and expecting to take more from it than by putting it on a card for the same purpose' " (15: 15). Small wonder that the indoor variety of gambling should have seemed but a natural corollary to the pick and shovel kind. Or that fatalism should have become a philosophy and equanimity a virtue.

Socially, the communities in the mining camps were conditioned by the nature of the employment. They were more or

6. Francis Brett Harte. *The Writings of Bret Harte*, 19 vols. (Boston: Houghton Mifflin Company, 1896–1906); 14: 41. In future references to this edition, the volume and page number will be given in the text.

less *de facto* and temporary. Random gatherings were formed and dispersed without achieving a higher form of organization than that established by mutual respect, a few mining laws, and the informal government of an *alcalde* or chief. Kin and custom, the bases of more stable communities in the East, were of less importance here. Also less available were any monitoring influences on truth, any readily obtainable checks on the veracity, experience, and general character of the applicant for a place in the group. In his study of the frontier, Ray A. Billington informs us that there "were [not] too many questions asked about the background of a newcomer; a glib young man could hang out his shingle as a lawyer after a few weeks of study and automatically become a member of the leadership elite."[7] Between such a "glib young man" and the confidence man who is a "quick study" for a new role, the difference is one of morality rather than of technique. Billington also tells of "two newcomers to a Kansas community, [who] agreed to address each other as 'General' and 'Colonel'; no one questioned their self-assumed ranks, but instead paid them such tribute that one became a senator and the other a social leader."[8] The naiveté of the average Westerner, his respect for titles real or nominal, his democratic tendency to give a man credit for whatever value he could live up to—these characteristics of the frontier obviously favored the enterprise of the confidence man. There is also a sense in which every man leaving the East to make a new man of himself arrived in the West as an impostor, a claimant for respect on the grounds of mere confidence.

According to Bret Harte, what replaced the bonds of the community was the ethic of the "partnership," with certain consequent adjustments in the ideas of social responsibility, honor, and justice. The individual, initially in the role of the "stranger," had first to satisfy not the social demands of a community—conformity in behavior, "useful" occupation—but the personal demands of each man dealt with as an individual—fairness improved by generosity, consideration warmed by loyalty. Chivalry reasserts itself as primarily a code of individual

7. Ray Allen Billington, *America's Frontier Heritage* (New York: Holt, Rinehart & Winston, 1966), p. 109.
8. Ibid., p. 100.

encounters and protective relationships. Thus, in *Cressy*, Harte makes it quite clear that community resentment against the schoolmaster necessarily takes second place to the formalities of a *duello* between Ford and Cressy's father or guardian. And of course Tennessee's partner proves that the offices of friendship are independent of and supersede the judgments of the community. Justice, then, ceases to have the long-term aspect which obtains in regular societies. In Boston or Philadelphia a crime may be cancelled, if at all, only by the acceptance of punishment involving isolation from society. But in Harte's West a past crime or a vague disparagement can be effectually cancelled by a present good deed or a demonstrable good quality. Thus a convicted horse thief, by responding appropriately to Salome Jane's kiss and by exhibiting a genuine love for horses, may be allowed to live happily ever after in possession of a beautiful wife and a prosperous stable. This is "California justice"; it is a judgment based on the immediate facts rather than on past history, on feeling rather than statute, and on the personal rather than the communal sense of a person's worth. These qualities of the West alter somewhat the context of the confidence man. In a looser society he is a freer agent. Also, his victims tend not to be specimens of generic mankind, vulnerable through their common share of human limitations such as vanity and greed. Instead they are individuals encountered under unique conditions. The "game" becomes a *duello*.

The first opponents are Ah Sin and Bill Nye. In the poem called "Plain Language from Truthful James," the "heathen Chinee," Ah Sin, "cons" the two miners temporarily by pretending to be ignorant of the card game they are playing. Thus Bill Nye is deluded into thinking he can cheat Ah Sin with impunity. A slight mistake betrays the fact that Ah Sin, too, is cheating. Bill Nye is of course disgusted and indignant, and all the more so because he has been outwitted by the man he thought was his dupe. What is really interesting here is Harte's manipulation of several contrasts between tone and action, between appearance and reality.

To begin with, Ah Sin appears "bland," "pensive," "childlike," and ignorant of the game of Euchre. He is in fact cunning, deceitful, and expert enough to cheat successfully for a long time.

Bill Nye appears to be a humorous hypocrite, cheating only inferior beings and becoming morally and patriotically aroused when it seems that Ah Sin has cornered the market in duplicity. Actually Bill Nye is at least as immoral as Ah Sin, and probably more reprehensible. Even the narrator is not quite what he seems. He appears and claims to be "truthful," "plain"-spoken, offended by Nye's cheating as well as by Ah Sin's. He presents himself as so disinterested that he takes no hand in the subsequent assault on the Chinaman and merely "remarks" on the case as an illustration of Asian behavior. This may be Harte's conception of James Gillis's deadpan style of humor, elsewhere described by Mark Twain. But to the reader this uninvolved narrator is still a player in the game; he is willing to let Ah Sin be cheated by Bill Nye, and he is ready to judge the Chinaman in racially prejudiced terms. The poem shows one "hand" but hints at another. The *real* players include (1) a representative white man whose corrupt ways the Chinese but imitate, (2) a mildly hypocritical sideliner who condemns himself in protestations of sincerity, and (3) a canny Chinaman whose bland face is as profoundly impersonal, racial, and self-protective as an almond-eyed mask.

Since Harte despised the poem as a bagatelle, it may be he did not realize that a happy chance had given him a potentially complex literary device—the device of the unconsciously self-condemning narrator. It was a device he never perfected in his prose, as Mark Twain did. But the poem owes its charm, as does Ah Sin, to a deceptive simplicity. The Chinaman remains an example of the confidence man whose "game" is to adopt the pose of the dupe. In doing so he tempts other men to reveal their cupidity and thereby achieves a moral victory of his own or, more properly, of the author's.

Much later, in a period of extreme dejection and financial insecurity, Harte wrote *The Story of a Mine*. His two attempts at drama had failed; he had written no short stories for three years; he was in Washington writing for a failing magazine (*The Capitol*) and surrounded as he thought by every species of corruption.[9] The first character he draws is a simple, childlike, and

9. George R. Stewart, *Bret Harte: Argonaut and Exile* (Boston: Houghton Mifflin Company, 1931), p. 241.

superstitious Mexican. His innocence is real and all too vulnerable. For the second character, Harte gives us Joseph Wiles, "a vagabond by birth and education, a swindler by profession, an outcast by reputation" (3: 6). It seems at first startling that the central word "swindler" should be embraced on two sides by words particularly associated with the two gamblers, the "vagabond" Jack and the "outcast" John Oakhurst. Like them Wiles is predatory, but he is soured and twisted beyond all resemblance. Everything about him is awry, as Harte explains in a patly Dickensian description: "He was a slight-built man with a dark, smooth face, that would have been quite commonplace and inexpressive but for his left eye, in which all that was villainous in him apparently centered. . . . Nature had apparently observed this, too, and had, by a paralysis of the nerve, ironically dropped the corner of the upper lid over it like a curtain, laughed at her handiwork, and turned him loose to prey upon a credulous world" (3:31). Wiles reminds us also of both Bill Nye and the heathen Chinee. Like Nye, he excuses his trickery on the basis of racial supremacy: "He did not scruple to cheat these Mexicans, they were a degraded race; and for a moment he felt almost an accredited agent of progress and civilization. We never really understand the meaning of enlightenment until we begin to use it aggressively" (3:6–7). This touch of political cynicism is worth noting. It does not, however, prevent Harte from perpetuating the ill fame of the degraded "Chinee"—for he tells us that "Wiles' right eye and *bland* face were turned toward the speaker" (italics mine; 3:10).

Meeting the simple-minded Concho in the hills, Wiles engages in what is obviously unequal combat. He learns that the Mexican and his two partners plan to have some of the local rock assayed on the chance that it might contain silver. Perceiving that Concho is unwary as well as ignorant, the con man immediately adopts the role of a metallurgist. With a guile reminiscent of Chaucer's Canon, he dazzles his victim by combining a silver nitrate solution with salt and getting a white precipitate of silver chloride. The display of elementary chemistry seems to Concho like magic, and thus it becomes mere chicanery. Wiles later performs a similar trick on Concho's friends: he melts a silver half-dollar into their specimen so that he may be sure of finding silver there when he tests for it. Only incidentally does he discover in the impromptu furnace the traces of mercury which tell him that the Mexicans have indeed stumbled onto valuable ground. They are of course unaware of it and he does not inform them. And so begins the series of deceptions and intrigues by which Wiles and others try to lay claim to the quicksilver mine. Forgeries and lawsuits are involved, but Wiles reappears for the closing acts in Washington, where he tries to lobby for Congressional support. He is aided by a pompous and immoral legislator named Gashwiler and a coquettish lady of fashion and intrigue somewhat resembling Laura in *The Gilded Age*. Ultimately he is defeated not by the law but by Concho's friend Carmen. The victory, as always, is on a personal basis. It is true that in this long *Story of a Mine* there is a tendency to see all scoundrels as ultimately in league with each other and exhibiting at least the illusion of solidarity and ubiquity. Temporarily the world is a convocation of scamps. But this is the sort of fantasy one might expect from a man pressed on all sides by debts and a recent history of failure.

In fact the story shows many of Harte's worst traits as a writer. The characters are inflated mannerisms, the plot is involved to no purpose: the tone is synthetically coy ("the astute feminine reader will of course understand...") or captiously cynical ("this National Absurdity was only equaled by another ..."), and the moral standpoint is uncertain. Joseph Wiles, one of the very few professed confidence men in Harte's writings, comes close to being a personification of those mundane practicalities and cheap dexterities which seem to triumph over the man who is innocent and deserving. There may be a self-indulgent bitterness in the creation of Joseph Wiles which prevents the portrait from having any real subtlety or significance.

How different is our impression of the Ingénue of the Sierras, that accomplished con woman, the antagonist of Yuba Bill. The story of Polly Mullins was written in 1893, during Harte's residence in the Van de Velde household in London. His biographer Stewart describes this period as one of "factory" production. Harte was able to turn out a steady line of stories of more or less uniform quality, although this quality was below that of his early work for the *Overland Monthly*. An air of futility and irony seems to have entered such late stories as *Cressy* and *Colonel Starbottle's Client*. Then, in *An Ingénue of the Sierras*, the familiar code of sentimental chivalry is turned inside out by a woman, and the result is a lively, tonic piece of writing.

The author identifies himself as a passenger on a stagecoach crossing Galloper's Ridge under Yuba Bill's charge. Thereafter the narrator accounts for himself among the "we" who provide the chorus for the action which follows. The crossing is a dangerous one. There is reason to expect that the stage will be "held up" by members of the Ramon Martinez gang. Yuba Bill's coolness is familiar but is accentuated by everyone's realization that the coach is traveling at breakneck speed on a narrow road. All do arrive safely at the way-station. But once there Bill orders a delay that mystifies the passengers. They do not know that he is disturbed by the fact that the stage was *not* robbed. Suddenly he challenges the one lady passenger with a direct question: "Did you signal to anybody from the coach . . . ?" The code of the West asserts itself in the passengers' reaction: "We all thought that Bill's courage and audacity had reached its climax here. To openly and publicly accuse a 'lady' before a group of chivalrous Californians, and that lady possessing the further attractions of youth, good looks, and innocence, was little short of desperation" (9:460–61). The bandit Martinez is forgotten in this surge of gentlemanly ardor. But, surprisingly, the young girl admits that she *did* signal. With growing animation and an engaging mixture of pride and defiance, she tells her story. She has run away from home, bringing with her the clothes with which her father had tried to bribe her to marry a man she hated. Instead she is now going to meet the man she loves so that they can be married in spite of all obstacles. She describes her lover as honest and brave, but poor and harried in his work as a collector of monies for a business firm. Does she remember the name of the firm? Yes, she thinks it is a Spanish name, something like Ramon Martinez. Her story ends in a determined burst of love and faith in her prospective husband, and then dissolves into tears of nervous exhaustion. The informal audience is embarrassed by her emotion but utterly subjugated by her appeal. She is a woman; she is a woman in distress; her distress is that of true love obstructed by a mercenary father; her love is innocent and it has the power to transfigure a highwayman into a deserving young man. On every count she scores infallibly. The passengers are ready to accept Bill's autocratic decision to allow the lovers to meet and even to marry on the spot if the groom will confess his true "business" and agree never to "work" for Martinez again. Everyone swears to put legal justice second to California justice and to keep faith with the lady.

It would seem as though Yuba Bill has again demonstrated the sagacity and tender-heartedness which make his tyranny acceptable and even morally refreshing. With his unerring eye he had detected the man in the brush by the roadside. He had pieced together the events which told that the girl must have signaled the outlaw. Finally, he had surprised the truth out of her. Convinced that her innocence was the sort that demanded protection, he had characteristically taken charge of the situation, even arranging to have the couple legally married. As he says of himself, "Speshul Providences take a back seat when [I'm] around." But now that the couple have actually departed and Bill is congratulating himself on his part in the affair, he learns that the man he has just allowed to escape is Ramon Martinez himself. The "innocent" girl was his accomplice in the theft of the baggage she was smuggling through as her own. Defeated by his own good intentions, Bill is yet able to reflect that he did not allow Martinez to escape entirely scot free. Whatever happens, "he's tied up to that lying little she-devil, hard and fast." But perhaps that is her ultimate success.

Her more immediate victory is primarily a humorous one. Lordly Bill is tricked into exerting his authority in behalf of a criminal. Chivalrous bystanders are tricked into acting as gentlemen in behalf of a liar and a thief. But her victory goes beyond the event. By using the identifying marks of the sentimental heroine as her camouflage, she proves just how superficial and trite they are. Equally factitious is her appearance of being "guileless as a child"; certainly anyone who has read *Cressy* should suspect this cliché. But in the tradition of all great liars, she molds her facts to the minds she is trying to impress. Whether or not she had prepared a story in case her signal was detected, she manages under the unexpected fire of Yuba Bill's questions to construct an acceptable context for herself and her actions. Like the famous lies of Huck Finn, her story borders on the truth, is internally consistent, and amply filled in with plausible detail. It is adjusted to the type of audience to which it is offered and flatters their conception of themselves as superior in worldliness. Although we may agree that she is a "lying little she-devil," we admire her courage, wit, and aplomb. Then, too, like the one woman who outwitted Sherlock Holmes, she gains honor through the prestige of her opponent.

Perhaps we are also relieved and attracted by Harte's satire on the conventions he elsewhere accepts. These conventions— the clichés of sentimentality—are in fact the staple ingredient of most of his fiction. "Serious" writers like Twain and Howells were not gentle in condemning him as a mere "purveyor of pathetics." Twain, in his *Autobiography*, claimed that Harte "had mastered the art of pumping up the tear of sensibility." It is the very metaphor, that of a mechanical pump, with which he describes the calculated sentimentality of the King and the Duke in *Huckleberry Finn*. The severest critics of Harte have seen him as a charlatan, relying on hackneyed formulas to evoke tears or smiles on demand. What, then, are we to think when Harte creates a con-woman protagonist who relies on the same hackneyed formulas to evoke a patronizing humor and a sentimental pity? Is he laughing at himself? At his audience? At his critics? These questions cannot be answered, but as they inevitably come to mind they increase the stature of the Ingénue. We should note, too, that unlike other less dubious alter egos of the author, she is not romantically idealized; she has neither the puerile innocence of George Barker nor the impossible charm of Mr. Jack Hamlin. But she does seem to know more about Francis Brett Harte.

Students of American literature are now accustomed to ignoring Stoddard's defense of Harte's realism and accepting Mark Twain's perhaps somewhat prejudiced view that it was he rather than Harte who knew life in the mines as it "really" was. Certainly Twain had the greater art to make this experience into literature, insofar as *Roughing It* is a greater book than *Tales of the Argonauts*. Gamblers as such do not appear to have played a large part in Twain's Nevada memories, but *Life on the Mississippi* does include "The Professor's Yarn" in which the Mississippi version of the Western gambler is finely presented.

John Backus is a steamboat gambler who begins his game many days before he comes to the table. Winning the confidence of the Professor, who is a fellow passenger on the boat, he throws out hints that he is a cattleman. Soon he becomes the epitome of a cattleman. All he knows is cattle, but about them he knows everything. He learns that the Professor is a surveyor and begins to envision a future partnership in which the boundary-maker and the cattle-supplier would profit from certain irregularities in the plumb line. Rebuffed by the Professor, he cheerfully directs the conversation into new channels. His prolixity is so engaging and his good humor so disarming that the Professor takes a friendly interest in him. Indeed Backus seems to require a guardian, for he at last succumbs to the repeated invitations of the professional gamblers to join them in a game. As he is traveling with considerable money and apparently knows little of cards, he seems an easy mark for the cardsharps. Concerned, the Professor watches the game and is even more disturbed to see the gamblers pressing the cattleman to drink. While he empties his glass in good faith, they covertly dispose of the contents of theirs. Soon their clear eyes see signs that the cattleman is befuddled. He is raising the stakes disastrously, irresponsibly high. With his natural buoyancy he continues to float at that precarious level. In another moment the gamblers expect to leave him high and dry. But when the cards are shown, the cattleman holds the winning hand and rolls over them, sweeping away all the money in sight. They are crushed and depressed as he towers above them, triumphant, exultant, and despite all the drinking he has done, perfectly sober. Only then does he announce that he is a professional gambler himself. Moreover, he is a confidence man.

Much later the Professor encounters him in a city street jauntily dressed in fashionable clothes. He is now willing to admit that he knows only as much about cattle as he could learn in two weeks in Ohio. Like the Ingénue, Backus had adopted the pose of countrified innocence and made a little knowledge go a long way. He proved himself even more of a master of circumstantial detail, pouring in fact after fact to swell the flood of confidences with which he deluged the Professor and washed away all distrust. He is one of hundreds of characters who demonstrate their author's love of the torrential talker, before whom the doubter is but a puny reed. Yet despite his volubility and the fact that he is more formidable than Ah Sin, he is really a less interesting character than the Chinaman or the Ingénue. His ruse is little more than a bluff which pays off as neatly as the climax to a practical joke. Like a number of Twain's early creations, he is a phenomenon without moral shadings.

It would be hard to claim much more circumstantial realism for the crafty John Backus than for the gentlemanly Jack Hamlin —both reveal as much about their creators' pet character types as they do about the "historical" West. Perhaps we can achieve a sense of perspective by glancing at George Devol's autobiography, *Forty Years a Gambler on the Mississippi*. In the "bad boy" tradition that Twain so loved, Devol boasts, "I guess I was about the worst boy of my age west of the Allegheny Mountains that was born of good Christian parents."[10] With the precocity of Simon Suggs he "could steal cards and cheat the boys at eleven; [and] stack a deck at fourteen." Thus runs the advertisement on the title page. The book itself is simply a long list of the con games that allowed him "to live off of fools and suckers." His story may not be literal fact in every detail, but it is instructive in its general tendencies. Devol is obviously proud not only of his success in duping victims but of his gentlemanly honor in taking only superfluous cash. There is a good deal of Jack Hamlin in the way he takes aside a young loser and returns his money with a lecture against gambling. Moreover, he keeps himself in good conscience by reflecting that his victims are usually those who think they are going to take an unfair advantage of *him*. Lacking the charm and interest of the fictional characters, Devol serves at least to underline the type itself, the gambler as con man.

In Harte's writings the type is developed most fully and prominently in the dual form of Oakhurst and Hamlin. They present the two sides of a romantic ideal, Oakhurst gathering to himself all the deep, stern mysteries of the impregnable man, while Hamlin sheds everywhere the sunny and debonair grace

10. George Devol, *Forty Years a Gambler on the Mississippi*, 2nd ed. (New York: George H. Devol, 1892), p. 10.

of the god-favored youth. Twain's gambler is closer to the Southern type of the humorous, "folksy," cunning manipulator—the quick-change artist of personal identities—who "lays" for his victim like a hunter in ambush. But, like the Byronic and Shelleyan versions of the Bret Harte ideal, he, too, makes gambling a philosophy as well as a profession, and handily turns to his own uses the speculative passion of the Gold Rush era.

CHAPTER THREE

And Back Again

Although Bret Harte gave the Far West a permanent if second-rate place in our literature, the first and perhaps only "Western" writer of first-rank stature was another member of the San Francisco literati. In this chapter we are going to be dealing for the first time with a major writer who used the confidence man extensively and differently at various stages of his own development. Mark Twain introduces us to a fully articulate West and he is a fully articulate man; hence, the uses of language become especially important to the consideration of Twain as a writer and the con man as a character.

In Bret Harte country men always distinguished between the few who "spoke well" and the many who did not, although of course it was believed that a man's value had little to do with his diction. Indeed, insofar as the Westerner felt his differences from the Easterner and was proud of them, he tended to foster his regional, dialectical, and slang-textured speech and to scoff at the imported, genteel, and more conceptual language of the professional man trained in the East. And yet—this language attracted him. He demanded it in his newspapers, and, as Billington has said, he demanded a newspaper almost as soon as he had a town with a name to bestow on one.[1] Albert H. Marckwardt, in a chapter of *American English* called "The Genteel Tradition and the Glorification of the Commonplace," points out that even the smallest of such towns might have its wooden "op'ry house" and its gilded "saloon" or "palace," courting cul-

---

1. Ray Allen Billington, *America's Frontier Heritage* (New York: Holt, Rinehart & Winston, 1966), p. 80.

ture with lumber and plate glass, enhanced by an opulent word.[2] There is, then, a sense in which the civilizing of the West was an effort of language, even at times an enterprise in which language took the place of a salable commodity. Among the vendors of rhetoric were of course the printer and the preacher who capitalized on a stock of ready-made phrases. But to say that the early word-peddlers were not always scrupulous, that they could exploit the naiveté of their customers, is not to deny that they were a part of the civilizing process.

Mark Twain, perhaps more than any other writer of the period, conveys to us the frontiersman's longing for an expanded emotional and intellectual life, and the humorously and pathetically vulnerable forms that this yearning takes. He is hungry for language. In his readiness to imagine great riches the provincial citizen is beguiled by the speculator whose words are gold-plated. In his eagerness for "elevation" he takes his newspaper for literature, his camp-meeting for religion, and his circus for drama. What this means is that he is the willing victim of the storyteller who is also an actor-showman, and above all a master of rhetoric, borrowed, stolen, or spontaneously generated. It also means that a particular relationship develops between the master of rhetoric and the people whom he addresses. In the following discussion of Twain's confidence men, I shall try to suggest the character of this relationship, the forms under which the confidence man operates, his obvious power as a controller of the imagination, his not so obvious function as a satirist of society, and his perhaps even less obvious condition as an exile from the hopes (however illusory) and the affections (however crass) of his fellow human beings.

On a small scale, we may begin with that combination of audacious idea and ingenious contrivance we call the practical joke. In Twain's writing there are innumerable examples of these miniature confidence games. As perpetrator he is not always aware of the moral character of what he is doing. He says in a reminiscent passage in the *Autobiography*, "In those extremely youthful days I was not aware that practical joking was a thing which, aside from being as a rule witless, is a base pastime and

2. Albert H. Marckwardt, *American English* (New York: Oxford University Press, 1958), pp. 111–13.

disreputable. In those early days I gave the matter no thoughts but indulged freely in practical joking without stopping to consider its moral aspects."[3] On the simplest level, these jokes are preverbal forms of the confidence game. For example, by means of an ingeniously folded sheet he confines hundreds of wasps in one side of a bed shared with a playmate named Jim. After first climbing into the "safe" side himself, he blows out the candle and lets Jim discover his bedfellows in the dark. The convulsive laughter which seizes the boy Clemens is hard for an adult to understand except on the primitive level of "slapstick" humor. It is interesting to note, too, that the whole idea flashes upon him like a "happy inspiration," but that he concludes by saying "any brainless swindler could have invented [it]."[4] The artist and the con man are brothers in technique, and both can enjoy being devils.

The very next chapter of the *Autobiography* tells of the visit of a "mesmerizer" to Hannibal in 1850, and of the boy Clemens's participation in a swindle of the public. The hypnotist claims that his subjects can react to stimuli while in a trance, and those who perform thus on the platform are objects of wonder and admiration in the eyes of the townspeople. Twain tells us that his motive for offering himself as a candidate is simply the desire to "be conspicuous and show off before the public." There seems to be no doubt, however, that an equally strong motive is the love of exercising his imagination, of calling upon it for spectacular effects. Consequently, he pretends to be hypnotized and to see visions and marvels that would defy any descriptive powers but his own. With a touch of Huck Finn's innocence, he fears that the showman will expose him as a fake. But he soon realizes that one con man will not betray another when their "games" are mutually profitable. Compunction does follow his success in conning the town; it is even increased by his discovery that a confession of the truth will not be believed. With chagrin, but with who knows how much uneasy pride, he finds that his power has isolated him and left him no outlet for shame.

3. Mark Twain, *The Autobiography of Mark Twain, Including Chapters Now Published for the First Time,* ed. Charles Neider (New York: Harper & Brothers, 1959), p. 48.

4. Ibid., p. 50.

How true the account itself is may of course be questioned, but its felt quality is verifiable; the love of personal display and dominance by means of "gaudy" rhetoric and colorful behavior is an essential part of Twain's psychological makeup and of the life of his fiction. So, too, is the sense of removal from the community at large.

It is almost natural that Twain should have combined such experiences of adolescent hoaxing with his early trades of printer and reporter. The famous literary hoaxes are indeed extensions of the practical joke in verbal form. *The Petrified Man* and *The Empire City Massacre* exhibit the same bravura imagination and yield the same kind of satisfaction to the author. It is a satisfaction roughly proportionate to the chagrin (present or prospective) of the audience that has been victimized. The difference is of course that the audience deserves its discomfort here—in the one case for its gullible attitude toward the "wonders of science," and in the other for its relish of brutality and violence. In a crude way we see here the social value of the confidence man; the hoax that succeeds because of unadmirable propensities in the victims has at least one moral dimension. As a literary device it has increasing importance for Twain as a critic of society.

But we cannot leave the discussion of practical jokes without noting the various instances in which Twain is the victim rather than the perpetrator. Very naturally he becomes morally indignant when the roles are reversed. One such experience occurs during his California days. After he has been ceremoniously presented with a meerschaum pipe, and after he has made a well-planned and touching "reply," he learns that his colleagues have given him a fake article and are amusing themselves over his elaborate speech. The feeling of shame lasts even after the jokers offer a genuine pipe and apologies.

A similar experience is described in the sketch called "How the Author was Sold in Newark." While Twain is on a lecture tour, a man comes to him and explains that he has an uncle whom nothing can entertain. Would the great humorist undertake to make him laugh or weep? He would. In the lecture hall that evening Twain looks for the old man and finds him sitting in the front row, with a stolid expression on his face. Twain begins his lecture, but no effort of his is successful; his jokes, his antics, his pathos, and his well-timed pauses are equally ineffective. Not a tremor passes over the old man's face. Later, of course, Twain learns that he is blind, deaf, and dumb. Appealing to us, Twain asks, "Now was that any way for the old man's nephew to impose on a stranger and orphan like me?"[5] Behind the exaggerated pathos there are traces not only of wounded personal pride, but of a jostled faith in humanity. The orphaned stranger in an unkind world is literally a description of Huck Finn and figuratively a description of the childlike and homeless Jim. In the relationship of these two waifs, the practical joke is revealed for what it really is—a cruel and heartless act which makes a mockery of trust and affection. Huck realizes he must apologize to Jim for the dream hoax he "plays" on him after the separation in the fog. When he does so, he is making his first step toward recognizing the human dignity of another individual and its proper claim on the heart. This lesson is one that Twain as well as Huck had to learn; it is one of the factors complicating Twain's attitude toward the glib (and morally careless) ingenuity of the confidence man.

When the "profit" ceases to be merely a laugh and becomes a sum of money, then we have moved from the realm of the practical joke to the realm of the confidence game. And we must begin with a look at the relationship between business and language. As the nineteenth-century American mind developed, it awakened to the idea of the personal fortune. One had only to listen to hear of "a good thing." Even Twain's Jim wanted to invest. Thus, when the pick and shovel days were over, a new era began, the day of the label, the trademark, the advertisement, the "spiel"—in fact, a new beginning for the word. It, too, was a prospecting tool. We must also consider that Twain's own conceptions and misconceptions about business underlay his presentation of the salesman. It would be hard to find a second American author of stature who took such interest in the practical business of selling his literature, or one who

---

5. Samuel Clemens, *Sketches*, in *The Writings of Mark Twain*, 37 vols. (New York: Gabriel Wells, 1922), p. 116. All future citations from Mark Twain's works will be taken from the volumes of this edition, unless otherwise noted.

undertook that venture with a more fatally romantic view of how wealth is produced. He seems to have thought it came into being in much the same way his stories did; that is to say, by means of a creative mind striking a happy thought, presenting it to advantage, and then monitoring the public's response by a word, a gesture, and a pause. After all, this was the way a fortune was made on the lecture circuit. The result should be a guaranteed laugh, an immediate profit. In fact Twain's favorite image of "working" the public, with its suggestion of pushing buttons and pulling stops, applies to both verbal and financial maneuvers. At times it can seem as though he believed the credit of the businessman to be only a function of the credibility of the storyteller. And, in Mark Twain's America, it must be admitted that when the frontiersman looked up from his plow, he was ready to listen to the marvelous; he was attracted as much by a present enrichment of the imagination as by the possibility of real wealth in the future.

Colonel Sellers, the least conscious of con men, knows this instinctively. At one point in *The Gilded Age* Sellers is convinced that the coming of the railroad will transform the few shacks and muddy waterside of Stone's Landing into a large and beautiful riverport city. He urges everyone to invest in a future city which he calls into being with a declarative sentence: "That's the place for the public square, courthouse, hotels, churches, jail—all that sort of thing. About where we stand, the deepo. . . . Down yonder the business streets, running to the wharves. The University up there, on rising ground, sightly place, see the river for miles."[6] Later on, when disgruntled laborers demand their pay for work done on the roadbed, he spellbinds them again with visions of the future. They cannot resist him until enough time has passed for their imaginations to cool down to the facts—and for the Colonel to seek friendlier company. Kenneth Lynn is perhaps the one major critic who has given a great deal of attention to the confidence man as an archetypal figure in American literature (along with the gentleman, the soldier, and the hunter). In his view Sellers is part of the tradition discussed in the first chapter of this book:

6. *The Gilded Age*, 1: 172.

Obviously bespeaking Twain's long acquaintance with the Confidence Man of the Southwestern tradition, Sellers re-enacts on a national stage Simon Suggs's back-country imitation of a well-heeled *homme d'affaires*, while his visionary description of a scheme for widening a tiny Missouri creek into the finest river in the West carries the loose-mouthed promotionalism of Joseph G. Baldwin's Ovid Bolus and "Blowing" Cave to new heights of floridity.[7]

But, as Lynn also recognizes, Sellers makes more of an appeal to our feelings: "In a world which glorified the conspicuous consumer and made a hero of the fast-buck operator Sellers was as much the victim as the victimizer.... Twain caught the pathos behind his mask ... the constant effort he made to avoid confronting the truth about himself" (Lynn, p. 179). That truth would presumably be the knowledge of his own failure, an admission that would be either a personal humiliation or a public insult to the land of plenty. And Sellers does have—in the hopeful way some men have a faith in a God—an unshakable confidence in the bounty of nature and the luck of events. But since he takes money on the basis of dreams that can never materialize, he is hard to distinguish from the confidence man. In short, he demonstrates the "business" of rhetoric and the power of language in a land of great hopes. Perhaps because he is almost never successful or perhaps because he is himself conned by the national temperament of optimism, he arouses no moral indignation. Our feelings are more akin to pity.

In general the art of lying for profit variously amuses, intrigues, and angers Twain, depending on the degree to which he either imaginatively or actually shares the feelings of the victim. Perhaps the simplest of such "games" is the mere act of substituting an imitation article for the real thing and using art or circumstance to sustain the illusion until the item is paid for. Such an exchange, one might almost call it an elementary form of the "switch," is the theft in *Tom Sawyer, Detective*. The criminal Jake confides to Tom: "It was a confidence game. We played it on a julery-shop in St. Louis.... We was dressed up fine, and we played it on them in broad daylight. We ordered the di'monds

7. Kenneth S. Lynn, *Mark Twain and Southwestern Humor* (Boston: Little, Brown & Company, 1959), p. 178.

sent to the hotel for us to see if we wanted to buy, and when we was examining them we had paste counterfeits all ready, and them was the things that went back to the shop when we said the water wasn't quite fine enough for twelve thousand dollars."[8] The jewelers have been imposed upon, but we do not feel their grievance very deeply. We are more impressed by the ingenuity of the thieves. It may be that we feel even some contempt for the businessmen who allow the appearance of fine clothes to overcome the precautions of good sense.

A more emphatic example of this kind of reaction against the victim in favor of the con man occurs in the story of "The Capitoline Venus." Here the criminal is a likable young American sculptor in Italy who needs money in order to marry the girl he loves. He is persuaded to make a statue on an antique model, to bury it, and then to "discover" it and claim the reward for finding a priceless relic of classical art. The hoax works perfectly. And we applaud its success. We do so because the victims are the kind of fool Twain delighted to satirize, especially in *Innocents Abroad*. They wish to be considered patrons of art, but they do not recognize what they admire unless it has first been labeled in a guide book or exhibited in a museum. Conversely, whatever is labeled as art they accept with unquestioning fervor. Such empty pretensions deserve to be cheated. The confidence game is clearly working as a tool of satire.

On the other hand, Twain knows a scoundrel when he sees one. On a Cincinnati steamboat in *Life on the Mississippi*, he overhears two drummers discussing their wares and the fraud they are practicing. One is marketing oleomargarine under the name and price of butter, and the other is bottling domestic cottonseed oil and labeling and selling it as imported olive oil. The "switches" here reflect Twain's most deprecating attitude toward business, according to which all enterprise is a "game" played by unscrupulous men, "the dollar their god, how to get it their religion."[9] Interestingly, he introduces the drummers as "brisk men, energetic of movement and speech," as though first reacting to those qualities that contrast most sharply with his own slow speech and delight in laziness. It is almost as though

8. *Tom Sawyer, Detective*, p. 152.
9. *Life on the Mississippi*, p. 328.

these men offend him primarily and precisely because they have qualities of the "go-getter" he never has had and never will have. However this may be, we should notice the importance of the printed label as a voucher for the real thing. Language, after all, is the result of an agreement to accept certain labels. The confidence man (like the writer) is only more systematic than other people in remembering this convention of trust.

Indeed, even such feelings as compassionate veneration or charitable pity can be invoked by the labels that describe those whom society has designated as its fallen heroes and its poor unfortunates. Thus when Twain is moved by a sight of the "Indians" at Niagara (*Sketches*), he is reacting to the marks of dress and appearance which spell "Indian." When he stops before a mendicant "Chinaman" in front of a tea merchant's establishment in New York City, he is again accepting the tokens of dress and feature which make the man a human sign or advertisement for the oriental drink. In both cases he reacts with more than ordinary feeling for the member of a downtrodden race. He venerates the Indian; he pities the Chinaman. Thus impelled, he speaks to the men and in both cases receives a jarring answer in a thick Irish accent. The labels were stamped on fake articles; the sentiment intended for the noble redman and the heathen Chinee is lost on Paddy and Mick. We laugh, as we are meant to laugh, at the sharp check given to Twain's sentimentality. Yet we feel, as we are meant to feel, the irony of substituting one stereotype for another, of hiring the much-bullied Irishman to impersonate fellow victims of intolerance. We have glimpsed pawns in a confidence game involving broad social forces and large-scale absurdities. But nearer at hand we have seen the alliance of the advertising sign and the side-show exhibit. P. T. Barnum comes to mind and so does the garb and placard of Jim as the "sick Arab" in *Huckleberry Finn*. The confidence man knows that the average person rarely questions the most freakish evidence that flatters while it accentuates his own sense of normalcy. He will believe in anything he is told to keep at arm's length.

With only a slight change in emphasis, I wish to consider now the more self-consciously artistic frauds in Twain's writings. Just as there is a characteristically American tension between speculation and implementation in the realm of business, there is in the realm of aesthetic enterprise a tension between the lure of imaginative fantasy and the love of factual detail. In the hands of the folk raconteur, fantasy and realistic detail combine to produce the tall tale and the humorous hyperbole. In the hands of an older Mark Twain they combine in the truthful lies of Huck Finn and the revealing games of such confidence men as Charles Williams (the "Burning Brand"), the King and the Duke of *Huckleberry Finn,* and the Connecticut Yankee. To deal with these characters effectively, it is helpful to divide artists of rhetoric into two categories. There are those like the Duke who falsify reality in print, and there are those like the King who do it in speech, on a real or a figurative platform.

Let us begin with the journeyman printer. He has a unique position in our history, being in many ways an intermediary figure between the artist who is free to express himself individually and the technician who is bound in ministry to a machine. Yet strangely enough it is the standardized operation of the printing equipment which frees the journeyman to travel from one location to another, always knowing that he can turn his hand to the trade whenever and wherever he chooses. The journeyman printer as self-made man has been immortalized in Franklin's *Autobiography.* Other histories of printers show a character less respectable and more itinerant—in short, a picaro. James G. Harrison makes this point in "A Note on the Duke in 'Huck Finn': the Journeyman Printer as a Picaro." In this article he mentions John Robb's John Earl and Henry Junius Nott's Thomas Singularity as predecessors of Mark Twain's Duke.[10] Earl has been discussed in an earlier chapter, where his quick wit and ready tongue were described as tools of the opportunist. Thomas Singularity is a less attractive but more interesting figure. We learn about him from a "friend" who writes the long, biographical preface to the "Odds and Ends from the Knapsack of Thomas Singularity, Journeyman Printer." Thomas is a foundling brought up by a wine merchant who gives the public adulterated wine in bottles with genuine

10. James G. Harrison, "A Note on the Duke in 'Huck Finn': The Journeyman Printer as a Picaro," *Mark Twain Quarterly* 8 (Winter 1947): 1–2.

stamps and labels. Thus the boy is early introduced to the art of misrepresentation in print. At fourteen he learns the intricacies of cards and dice and uses them to good advantage while pretending to heed the religious scruples of the master of the printshop. The writer of the preface records the frequent debauches and frequent disappearances of Thomas, after which he usually reappears at a later date and in a different town bearing the marks of his strenuous and irregular adventures. His very surname, Singularity, attests to the fact that he was conceived in the tradition of the "original" character, and his immorality is excused with mock seriousness as the byplay of genius. Like Burns, Sheridan, and Fox, he cannot be restricted by the "cold and calculating rules of speculative morality."[11] He is a braggart, an egotist, and a clever though self-deluded man. We should also note that he shares a professional bond with such men as Bret Harte, Sam Clemens, and W. D. Howells.

In some of the remarks made by these ex-printers, the character of the journeyman develops further toward that of the Duke. Howells, for example, points out the relationship between the old-fashioned printer and the popular theater: "It was Shakespeare who was oftenest on our tongues; indeed, the printing-office of former days had so much affinity with the theater that compositors and comedians were easily convertible; and I have seen our printers engaged in hand-to-hand combats with column-rules, two up and two down, quite like the real bouts on the stage."[12] It has long been known that Shakespearian travesties were popular in the West; it appears that the Duke's fondness for the "blood-curdling broad-sword conflict in Richard III" may have been a weakness that came with his trade. Apparently he thought he could get audiences to pay for printing-room horseplay.

An even more revealing comment on the Duke may be found in a speech Twain gave before the Typothetae Dinner commemorating Benjamin Franklin's birthday. The speech was given on January 18, 1886, less than a year after the publication

11. Henry Junius Nott, *Novelettes of a Traveller* (New York: Harper & Brothers, 1834), 1: 23.
12. W. D. Howells, *Impressions and Experiences* (New York: Harper & Brothers, 1896), p. 23.

of *Huckleberry Finn*. Like that book it describes an outmoded way of life in nostalgic terms: ". . . the tramping 'jour' . . . flitted by in the summer and tarried a day, with his wallet stuffed with one shirt and a hatful of handbills, for if he couldn't get any type to set he would do a temperance lecture. His life was simple, his needs not complex; all he wanted was plate and bed and money enough to get drunk on, and he was satisfied." [13] The Duke, too, has a hatful, or rather a trunkful, of handbills, and in them the various roles he has played as a confidence man are identified and labeled. He is Dr. Armand de Montalban, a phrenologist; he is Garrick the Younger, a tragedian; and he is a host of other gloriously titled impostors. Not only can he recreate himself out of paper and ink, but he can reidentify Jim also, by means of a spurious handbill. We never know his true name; nor does it seem likely that any combination of letters could have more legitimacy than another in registering him in a ledger of births. His definitive characteristics are rather his mobility, his singularity, his willingness to profit by his fellow man's desire to get a bargain rate, a cheap titillation, a mean revenge. His ideas run to bizarre mutations of the real thing, to travesties of the recognizable. In his hands nothing is assured of its integrity; everything can be disfigured, until even language becomes grotesque in the bleatings of "William Wilks." In a book about freedom, his irresponsibility becomes more than the stock characteristic of a journeyman printer. He is a foil for Huck. The kind of freedom the Duke enjoys is the expression of antisocial impulses, while the freedom Huck enjoys is the expression of personally chosen loyalties. As a confidence man the Duke is a journeyman printer turned loose on the world. He lives by the cynical wisdom and practical ingenuity of the shop as well as by its irreverent prankishness and its bare-faced assumption of familiarity with literature and knowledge in general. Totally individualistic, he always conceives of himself as separate from the members of the community, whether he happens to be "taking them in" or they happen to be driving him out. He occupies a printing shop only once and then only as a temporary stand-in for the Pokeville editor. His society has no

13. *Speeches*, p. 140–41.

office for him. But he survives. And he has much to do with our opinion of a society venal enough to support him.

Like the printer, the public speaker is in a special position of authority with words. Instead of a press he uses a platform, and thereby associates himself with the showman and the exhibitor. As we saw in the first chapter, most backwoods audiences were willing to swallow a large dose of the incredible if it looked, smelled, and tasted like undeniable fact. They cherished the tall tale and crowded to see the freakish animal which was living proof of the inconceivable. A lie had only to sound like a literal report to be accepted. If he had not already known that this was true of his own time and place as well, Twain learned it in his escapade on the mesmerist's platform. When he himself presided before audiences, he often used a rhetoric of artful hyperbole and made his appearance as striking as possible. This background should be kept in mind as we review several confidence men who speak and cavort on real or imaginary platforms.

The threshold of Twain's door is one such platform. There the echo-salesman delivers his long story in "The Canvasser's Tale" and tries to persuade the author to buy an echo. A flowery, saccharine tale is unfolded, involving an uncle who collected echoes and ending with the sad plight of the speaker, who would be so grateful to anyone who invested in the connoisseur's stock he is peddling. Just as one good craftsman must admire another, so one good liar must appreciate the skill and merit of another. Twain satirizes the "salespitch" in this bit of fanciful hokum, but at the same time he honors it by taking delight in the fluency and fecundity of the imagination behind it. There is, one might almost say, a fraternity of the platform.

This attitude can also be seen in the chapter of *Life on the Mississippi* called "A Burning Brand." The hero of this episode is also its villain; he is a Harvard graduate and a social outcast, a minister's son and a daring burglar, and, at the time of the story, a consumptive inmate of the state penitentiary. His platform is at first merely figurative. Using a fictitious name, Joe Hunt, and imitating the style of an illiterate ex-burglar, he writes a long letter addressed to himself, Charles Williams. In the letter "Joe Hunt" refers to himself as a former inmate and friend of Williams's. Now that he is free in the outside world, he is writing to Williams to thank him for having moved him to Christian beliefs by religious teachings and pious example. It is to these influences that Hunt attributes his desire to shun crime and begin life anew. With the help of fortuitous accidents, model prayers, and a benign benefactor, he declares that he has become everything a clergyman could desire in a repentant sinner. In conclusion, he lavishes affectionate concern on Williams, remembering that Williams had come near to dying of tuberculosis. After a few more sugary phrases, the letter ends.

Improbable, sickly sweet, the letter is still nothing less than a considerable literary achievement, for it is an ingenious compendium of sentimental-religious clichés—essentially that of the "hard case" melting in the sun of a benefactor's trust and the blessings of honest labor and Sunday school classes. The letter also illustrates a clever use of a persona established and maintained by a distinctively illiterate and simple-minded rhetoric which mixes the diction of prison slang with the jargon of the pulpit. And, as Twain notes with unconcealed admiration, the "nub" of the letter, its raison d'être, is the artfully unobtrusive reminder that Hunt's good friend Williams is still in prison with a bleeding lung. The letter is a magnificent superstructure built for the sole purpose of justifying its cornerstone, a covert appeal to the emotions. Williams hopes that his readers will pity him enough to work for his release from prison.

The subsequent history of the letter is the story of a far-reaching abuse of confidence. The document is smuggled out of the prison and into the hands of charitable ladies who Williams hopes will campaign in his favor. From them it travels the rounds of many churches where it is read from the pulpit (or platform). Invariably the listeners are "pumped" dry of all tears and become inert with sympathy. When publicly read the letter has almost the same effect as one of the King's speeches in *Huckleberry Finn*; it reduces the mass of people to identical machines which can be worked like pumps when they are well greased with "soul butter." After a suspicious literary man (identified as Charles Dudley Warner) suggests that the letter is *too* neatly constructed, application is made to the prison warden and the fraud is uncovered. Those who have been "conned" are ashamed, but Twain's exasperation is tinged with respect for a fellow practitioner in the art of fiction: "... it was the confoundedest, brazenest, ingeniousest piece of fraud and humbuggery that was ever concocted to fool poor confiding mortals with! The letter was a pure swindle, and that is the truth. And take it by and large, it was without a compeer among swindles. It was perfect, it was rounded, symmetrical, complete, colossal!"[14] In the struggle between moral and aesthetic judgments, the latter seems to have won out. Nor should this fact surprise us, for it is obvious that Williams's real accomplishment is close to Twain's own in *Huckleberry Finn*. Like Twain, Williams constructs a first-person narrative approximating colloquial speech (stilted and self-conscious, to be sure) and, like Twain's "bad" King, he uses the clichés of the Sunday school to take advantage of and indirectly to satirize the sentimental weakness of the "good" people. Even in his enforced isolation from society, the educated burglar has the power to show up that society as dupes of mere rhetoric and to arouse the spontaneous admiration of a fellow artist who shares his contempt for the audience.

But of course Williams is only an intelligence with a name. The self-styled King of France is one of Twain's most richly embodied characters. His "line" of work includes temperance lecturing, doctoring, preaching, and "missionaryin['] around"— all of which play upon man's eagerness to substitute a short emotional enthusiasm for a prolonged effort of will. Like Twain's "jour" printer, who also preaches on temperance in order to get money for his drink, the King enters the story pursued by a disillusioned crowd who have discovered his secret fondness for the bottle:

... somehow or another a little report got around last night that I had a way of puttin' in my time with a private jug on the sly. A nigger rousted me out this mornin', and told me the people was gatherin' on the quiet with their dogs and horses, and they'd be along pretty soon and give me 'bout half an hour's start, and then run me down if they could; and if they got me they'd tar and feather me and ride me on a rail, sure. I didn't wait for no breakfast—I warn't hungry.[15]

14. *Life on the Mississippi*, p. 421.
15. *Huckleberry Finn*, pp. 168–69.

The fate so narrowly escaped this time is reserved for him at the end of the book. Significantly, Huck replaces the Negro as the person who delivers the humane warning—but this time it comes too late. Always until this denouement the threat of expulsion remains in the air. Some form of violent ostracism is inevitable, for the King leads people to expose their gullibility and this is a service rarely forgiven. What the audience at the temperance lecture does not understand is that the rhetorically induced vision of the evils of drink has nothing to do with the King's taste for liquor. Being but empty verbiage, it is neither enhanced nor despoiled by the private act. However, to admit the dissociation would be to admit the power mere word-formulae have over them, and so the citizens quite naturally choose to honor the words and reject the man.

Initially, however, the King is a complete success. He gives the public exactly what it wants. On the platform of the camp-meeting he personifies a stereotyped figure of Sunday school literature—the reformed sinner. By claiming to be a former pirate he also appeals to a cheaply romantic love of the exotic and the glamourous. Then he flatters the crowd by suggesting that they are worthy to receive the spiritual credit of sending him as a missionary to other pirates—expenses paid. Because the King's diction is familiar ("a changed man," "the true path," "benefactors of the race," etc.), he is taken on trust.

The relationship between the control of language and the control of confidence is even more obvious in the Wilks episode. There the sentimental twaddle Huck calls "rot and slush" is actually as strong as a net thrown over and incapacitating the common sense of the townspeople. So strong is the whole fabric of this speech, that is to say, so well is it suited to the mentality of the listeners, that it can make the isolated word "orgies" into an acceptable substitute for "obsequies." Only one man present has a vocabulary large enough to include both words; he is also the only man with intelligence and humanity enough to penetrate the sham sentiment and to see the real harm it may do.

Dr. Robinson's first response to the King is a sudden burst of laughter at the complete absurdity of his "English" accent. The reasonable mind must see the King as a buffoon here, although he is not consciously playing the part of one. However, when occasion calls for it, he is not above such deliberate clowning as the Royal Nonesuch. In that episode he becomes part of the tradition of animal exhibits and freak shows, as well as of simple low comedy. Professor B. J. Whiting has suggested various antecedents for the "camelopard," particularly the hoax of the Guyuscutus, a much-advertised "monster" which conveniently breaks loose after an audience has gathered and paid to see it.[16] Interesting, too, in this regard is a minor sketch of Poe's called "Four Beasts in One; the Homo-Cameleopard," published in the *Southern Literary Messenger* in March, 1836, and reprinted elsewhere numerous times. In this story Poe takes us back in time to the ancient city Antiochus beside the broad river Orontes. The city, doomed to be destroyed eventually by earthquakes, even now in its splendor contains "an infinity of mud huts, and abominable hovels. We cannot help perceiving abundance of filth in every kennel, and, were it not for the overpowering fumes of idolatrous incense, I have no doubt we should find a most intolerable stench."[17] It is the day of a great festival, and tamed animals walk the streets with the mob, all waiting for the appearance of Antiochus Epiphanes, King of Syria. At last, fresh from the slaughter of "a thousand chained Israelitish prisoners" (a slaughter of the innocents), he grandly shows himself—but in the shape of a grotesque cameleopard. He is hounded by the animals of the city, but crowned with laurel by its citizens. One would like to think that Twain knew this story, and indeed Walter Blair, in *Mark Twain & Huck Finn*, raises the question and leaves it open. Whatever its background, the spectacle in *Huckleberry Finn* of the ring-striped and spotted old man prancing naked on the stage is as pitiful as it is comic. We have no indication that he feels the degradation, but we do know that Twain wrote to Howells at one time that his own role as a humorist sometimes made him feel he was painting himself striped in order to make a (perhaps shameful) exhibit of himself.

The King's last "game" is another staging of the Royal None-

16. B. J. Whiting, "Guyuscutus, Royal Nonesuch and Other Hoaxes," *Southern Folklore Quarterly* 8 (December 1944): 251–75.

17. Edgar Allan Poe, *Complete Works of Edgar Allan Poe*, ed. James A. Harrison (New York: Fred De Fau and Co., 1902), 2: 205–6.

such in the town near the Phelps plantation; but this time the populace has been forewarned, the rancor of past victims catches up with the "poor pitiful rascals" and drives them out of town on a rail. It is at this point that Huck says, "Human beings *can* be awful cruel to one another."[18] The humbuggery of these confidence men is a lesser offense against humanity than the brutal vengeance that casts them out of society.

In looking back over the development of the King and Duke as characters, one can see this moral perspective opening up gradually. The first confidence game, the camp-meeting appeal for funds to convert pirates, "takes in" a large but anonymous crowd and costs each individual a trifling sum of money. In the Royal Nonesuch performances a more specifically characterized audience loses a small sum but considerable dignity. In both cases the losers rate little sympathy, since it is their own weak foolishness or base curiosity which leads them into the trap. In the Wilks episode there is again a group of people whose delusions are deserved; but there are a few individuals who are particularly cheated, who are conspicuously innocent, and who lose or almost lose a great deal of money. The Wilks girls are still really children; they are members of the weaker sex; thus Huck shows an unconscious chivalry as well as a clear-headed perception of their goodness when he pities them and foils the "game" which would have left them destitute. His resolution to do so begins to form after Mary Jane chides her sister for calling Huck a liar: "It don't make no difference what he *said*—that ain't the thing. The thing is for you to treat him *kind*, and not be saying things to make him remember he ain't in his own country and amongst his own folks."[19] She turns this into a modified Golden Rule when she says: "If you was in his place it would make you feel ashamed; and so you oughtn't to say a thing to another person that will make *them* feel ashamed."[20] Here we must remember Twain's description of himself as "a stranger and orphan" put to shame in Newark, New Jersey, and hear also an echo of Jim's sad reproach to Huck: "Trash is what people is dat puts dirt on de head er dey fren's en makes 'em

18. *Huckleberry Finn*, p. 321.
19. Ibid., p. 242.
20. Ibid.

ashamed."[21] If there is a fraternity of platform rhetoricians, there is also a fraternity of the orphans and strangers whose chagrin is the knowledge of ostracism, the ache of all suffering. Once Huck identifies himself with the orphaned girls, the King and Duke for the first time lose our smiling complicity.

They forfeit even more of our tolerance when they abscond with Jim. By this act the King and Duke put themselves in opposition not to a foolish multitude, nor even to a few innocent girls, but to the highly individualized central character of the book, with whom we are in complete moral sympathy. Here the confidence men are clearly no longer just instruments of satire with whom we may share a laugh. They are business partners with a society that deserves only contempt.

I cannot, therefore, agree entirely with Kenneth Lynn's view that the King is a "freak," that he is "outside the society he gulls, and [that] therefore Huck's disapproval of him is not a comment on the population of the Happy Valley" (Lynn, p. 225). It seems to me that the isolation of the two con men is not due to a qualitative difference in morality. The difference is in the degree of skill and imagination with which these men are able to turn the venality of others to their own advantage. The King and Duke can outwit the majority of the populace for a time. But their cunning is a pitiful weapon against educated intelligence and only a temporary protection against the brute strength of a townful of victims.

Thus, when some time has elapsed and Jim has been found, Huck's widely tolerant and deeply humane pity can extend once more over the King and Duke. In their final hour we are prevented from judging them too harshly by having our attention called instead to the mob's capacity for cruelty. In retrospect we may see a pattern to the King's "operations" which suggests that money is only part of the subsistence he gains from his appeals for confidence. His method in each case is to present a woebegone appearance, and to claim a great misfortune and an exemplary piety (or dignity); the inevitable result is a rush of pity which he converts into coin or privileged position. The feeling so aroused is not of course true sympathy; it is rather the sensation of sympathy which, like the rhetoric of religion,

21. Ibid., p. 119.

impinges on the ear and activates the tear ducts without ever coming close to the heart. Yet it is an expression of interest, an act of embracing the individual into the arms of the community if only for a brief and insecure period of time. In one sense, asking for attention and receiving it under false pretenses may be less humiliating than asking for it and being rejected in one's own person. Many of Twain's own antics can be viewed in this light. He, too, had experienced the rhythm of community acceptance and rejection, and could find it natural to pity those who were more outcast than Huck.

The social status of the confidence man rises and the scale of his significance enlarges in *A Connecticut Yankee in King Arthur's Court*. Here Twain allows a mere human being to "con" a whole society and to get away with it for almost a lifetime. He gives this destiny to a brisk and buoyant mechanic whose acumen is Yankee American, but whose spirit is essentially Western. The Yankee invents machinery, the Westerner invents a country. We have seen Colonel Sellers conjure up a town, and his voice is an echo to Hank Morgan's initial enthusiasm: "Look at the opportunities here for a man of knowledge, brains, pluck, and enterprise, to sail in and grow up with the country." [22] These words, so often spoken with a face toward the virgin West, are now addressed to an old, old land at a time when it is just about to see the beginning of a new Western civilization —Christian Europe. The contrast between sixth-century England and nineteenth-century America provides an unusual amount of gratuitous humor, but the hidden likenesses are the serious matter of the book. King Arthur and his nobles are like privileged castes anywhere; the degraded peasants are like all those who suffer under a monarchic government, an established church, a self-perpetuating ignorance. The Yankee's response is: "Certainly a superior man like me ought to be shrewd enough to contrive some way to take advantage of such a state of things." [23] This is the language of the mechanical expert, the reformer, and the confidence man. In fact the optimism of the earlier section of the book is the result of faith in the power of mechanical engineering, added to enthusiasm over the pros-

22. *A Connecticut Yankee in King Arthur's Court*, p. 60.
23. Ibid., p. 37.

pect of recreating England in the image of her colony. Then, for a time, it seems as though England has remade the Yankee in the image of Merlin, the arch confidence man.

To "beat him at his own game," the Boss stages miracles with Fourth of July fireworks, but with "style" and "effect" that the Mississippi King would have envied. Confidence, as he learns very early, is extended to everyone and to everything. This is the age of miracles and tall tales, eremites and dragons. To confront a progressive, fact-loving, gadget-minded Yankee with a backward, fact-shunning, marvel-oriented world is perhaps the ultimate recognition of the tension between fantasy and actuality. Here of course the tension provides both a literary approach and a factor in the plot. Indeed the strain of authenticating the paradox in the title has been observed by those critics who dislike the book, who think it elaborately immature. But for our purposes we must realize that Twain has created, on a scale larger than ever possible in the American West, an opportunity for one man to con a multitude.

Hank Morgan has that blend of " 'cuteness" and conscience (which latter he despises as heartily as Twain) that allows him to be a confidence man but forces him to be a reformer. What he finds is a country that can bind him in chains but which is itself pinioned and swathed in superstition. The situation might be described in words from Twain's first look at a portion of Europe: "We were in the heart and home of priestcraft—of a happy, cheerful, contented ignorance, superstition, degradation, poverty, indolence, and everlasting, unaspiring worthlessness."[24] But Twain then added: "And we said fervently, It suits these people precisely; let them enjoy it, along with the other animals, and Heaven forbid that they be molested."[25] Hank does indeed molest Arthurian England, at first because he must do so to preserve his life. Later he is moved by indignation. He, too, sees human beings reduced to the level of animals because they do not use soap, or even arithmetic. In the episode of the enchanted castle Hank watches in astonishment as Sandy embraces the highborn "ladies" she has saved with his help. They are literally hogs rescued from a pigsty, but Hank must pretend that the

24. *Innocents Abroad*, p. 268.
25. Ibid.

shapes he sees are the result of an enchantment, and that to all other eyes the swine are human beings. The association of hogs with moral and intellectual sloth occurs also in *Huckleberry Finn* in the river towns where "hogs loafed and grunted around everywheres." When the Yankee says, "I was ashamed of her, ashamed of the human race," he is echoing Huck Finn. But he is not an ignorant, self-doubting boy like Huck; nor is he a transient caricature like the Clemens of *Innocents Abroad*. Once he understands that he is in the sixth century to stay, he becomes an entrepreneur in civilizations. Discreetly he introduces various forms of training and education to provide him with knowledgeable assistants. He confides that "I meant to work this racket [secret preparation] more and more as time wore on, if nothing occurred to frighten me." [26]

His primary advantage in this enterprise is his knowledge of mechanical cause and effect and his imaginative, dramatic use of platform technique. In one such display, the miracle of the restored fountain, he uses an iron pump to bring a gush of water from a sacred font, and thus to bring a gush of tears from the grateful and adoring crowd. It is a situation the King would have appreciated; he himself was limited to a metaphorical "pumping" of sentiment. But for all Hank's dependence on machinery and his use of mechanical metaphors—Sandy, for instance, is a conversation-mill that never needs repairs—his New England heritage disdains the idea of men as composites of levers and wheels. In a statement full of typical irony, the reformer tells a courageous young man and woman: "I'll book you both for my colony; you'll like it there; it's a Factory where I'm going to turn groping and grubbing automata into *men*." [27] The idea of using a factory to change machines into men, of using mass-production techniques to turn out individuality and initiative, is certainly humorous. But it is also a sign of desperation in the author; Twain knows how soon his character is going to be overwhelmed by the forces he is fighting.

The Yankee's defeat is made inevitable by the larger machinery of history. From one point of view it is understandable that his brand of civilization should have died out, and it is a doubt-

26. *Connecticut Yankee*, p. 79.
27. Ibid., p. 47.

ful blessing that it should have been "reborn" in nineteenth-century America. For what is Hank's science but mechanical ingenuity, electrical wiring, and explosives? What does it build at last but a huge engine of death? His culture is a lead-pencil and newsprint variety, addicted to wall-chromos and needle-point sentiment. Politically, it is true, his ideas are egalitarian and republican; but they naively assume an electorate of idealized men, all of whom have gone through the Man Factory process. In the end Hank is inadequate to the task of uplifting a people whose minds are enchanted and enslaved. He and they do not understand the same thing by labels such as "dignity" and "freedom." All that they understand, and all that he can finally provide, is a purely mechanical spectacle. The failure of the enterprise of language—and of civilization—occurs as Hank, conjuring over the multitude, enunciates the garbled letters of the "unpronounceable" name.

As the ultimate showman, he is still wasting his breath (as no doubt Twain himself thought that *he* was), for even after Hank has made corpses of his enemies, their rotting bodies will destroy him. Homeless on earth and in time, the Yankee mechanic dies not once but three times. Bernard De Voto has written at length about the morbid fantasies of loss and exile which filled page after page during the later years of the author's life. Twain's growing conviction that man's free will is negligible would seem antithetical to the spirit of nineteenth-century America. It is also incompatible with the further delineation of the confidence man, who is himself a man who devises schemes, a man who chooses the roles he will play. In the end, in *The Mysterious Stranger*, all options revert to Satan, language is silenced, and confidence in life is withdrawn.

PART II

Inveigling the Spirit

CHAPTER FOUR

From the Other World

As we enter the second half of this study, we shall have to recognize, as Twain did, the cultural preeminence of the East; we shall have to follow him back to the rich literary world of New England, where the life of the spirit had been going on for a century. We shall then see uses of the confidence man that are not so much humorous and regional as philosophical, allegorical. Of course, the "games" will still be played for money. But they will be conceived in the subtler terms of emotional longings, aesthetic needs, and spiritual hopes. In particular, the present chapter will be devoted to an area of speculation that drew as many false claimants as the mining districts of the West—and began to do so much earlier. This is the area of supernaturalism, of bizarre faiths and the hunger of the average man for assurances from "the other world."

In New England we will find Hawthorne early working on the problem of man's legitimate spiritual hopes. The struggles which fascinate him are those in which the individual saves or damns his immortal soul by preserving or losing his fellowship with men. Only a confidence man could urge self-sufficiency. If he did so, he would be a smiling temptor, a false father like the Devil in *Young Goodman Brown*. And here we have a beginning for the identification of the con man with the Principle of Evil which is behind almost every example we shall subsequently meet.

According to Hawthorne the failure to see other human beings as individuals with souls of their own leads to the Swedenborgian sin of manipulation, the imposing of one's own will on

another person. This evil results in the loss of the victim's autonomous existence, his responsibility to God. Perhaps the most
dramatic form of such usurpation is the case of the "spiritualist"
who arranges to use (and display) another person as a "medium." In *The Blithedale Romance* (1852), in *The Undiscovered
Country* by Howells (1880), and in *The Bostonians* by James
(1886), a character claiming supernatural authority utterly dis-
possesses and claims for his own use the soul of a helpless girl
and more or less purposely deludes the public into thinking her
the medium of spiritual communication.

In *The Blithedale Romance*, Westervelt is an unscrupulous
stage-manager and "promoter" who makes Priscilla into an
exhibit, with no more regard for her personal integrity than he
would have for the "soul" of a crystal ball. In his use of a mysterious and satanic power, in his love of planned indirection, and
in his highly developed instinct for meddling, he resembles the
lurid Carwin of C. B. Brown's *Wieland*.[1] Both these villains
emerge from the bizarre realm of the Gothic "chiller," both play
the theme of clairvoyance on the instrument of virgin woman-
hood. Though Carwin is a literal "biloquist" (or ventriloquist),
Hawthorne's Devil figure—like any other confidence man—also
speaks in at least two voices. Yet Westervelt has none of the
tragic ignorance and final remorse that partially extenuate the
guilt of Carwin. He is indeed less of a human being and more of
a deliberate artifice; he combines Zenobia's flair for exotic appearances and dramatic effects, Hollingsworth's readiness to
dominate other souls for his own purposes, and Coverdale's detached interest in other lives as the material for recreation—that
is, for both amusement and for reconstruction through artifice.
Westervelt is clearly a Devil figure. This is a thesis William
Bysshe Stein develops in his book, *Hawthorne's Faust*.[2] Of the
confidence men we have discussed he is probably the best physical embodiment of the high coloring, pretentious manner, and
ingratiating air which usually characterize the spoken rhetoric

1. Charles Brockden Brown, *Wieland; or, The Transformation. An
American Tale* . . . (New York: T. & J. Swords, 1798).
2. William Bysshe Stein, *Hawthorne's Faust: A Study of the Devil
Archetype* (Gainesville: University of Florida Press, 1953), pp. 126–28.

of the con man. Quite naturally, his patent falsity first reveals itself in physical terms:

In the excess of his delight, he opened his mouth wide, and disclosed a gold band around the upper part of his teeth; thereby making it apparent that every one of his brilliant grinders and incisors was a sham. This discovery affected me very oddly. I felt as if the whole man were a moral and physical humbug; his wonderful beauty of face, for aught I knew, might be removeable like a mask; and, tall and comely as his figure looked, he was perhaps but a wizened little elf, gray and decrepit, with nothing genuine about him, save the wicked expression of his grin.[3]

In fact it is this preternatural grin which marks him as a confidence man. Poe, in "Diddling Considered as One of the Exact Sciences," explains that "your *true* diddler winds up all with a grin. . . . He grins when his daily work is done . . . a diddle would be *no* diddle without a grin."[4] Though perhaps unaware of this truism, Coverdale *is* suspicious of Westervelt from the start. Later, hearing Westervelt's spiel on the public platform, he judges it in terms that condemn both the vogue of spiritualism and the cynicism of all con men who appeal in one way or another to the religious instinct: "It was eloquent, ingenious, plausible, with a delusive show of spirituality, yet really imbued throughout with a cold and dead materialism."[5] Westervelt is the fiend who wears the mask of the charmer. He ruthlessly manipulates those in his power and toys with the curiosity and soul-hunger of others. He is even capable of amused detachment and moral impenetrability at the issue of his own defeat. The fact that he survives with only a temporary and incidental loss of power suggests that, like Melville's Confidence Man, he is only the current manifestation of an enduring principle of evil.

His victims are in general the public and specifically the two women whose lives he has contaminated. Zenobia has the strength to resist his will and to break from him, but only at a

3. Nathaniel Hawthorne, *The Blithedale Romance and Fanshawe* (Columbus: The Ohio State University Press, 1964), p. 95.

4. Edgar Allan Poe, "Diddling Considered as One of the Exact Sciences," in *Complete Works of Edgar Allan Poe*, ed. James A. Harrison (New York: Fred De Fau & Co., 1902), 5: 213.

5. *The Blithedale Romance*, p. 200.

terrible cost. She has had to develop and exert an energy for which she can find no subsequent outlet except in perfervid "causes," an unwise love, and a theatrical suicide. At the other extreme, Priscilla has no strength of assertion, but infinite powers of response. In the climactic scene in which she stands between the malignant call of Westervelt and the benevolent call of Hollingsworth, she is simply drawn by the greater magnetism. And yet, we believe, her going is voluntary and based on her past associations with a man who has shown her true, if unthinking, kindness. In Priscilla a good instinct has prospered where before only a dead will obeyed. Hawthorne shows the full extent of the diabolical function he has given his confidence man when he has a skeptical member of the audience discuss the implications of the Veiled Lady phenomenon:

Human character was but soft wax in his [Westervelt's] hands; and guilt, or virtue, only the forms into which he should see fit to mould it. The religious sentiment was a flame which he could blow up with his breath, or a spark that he could utterly extinguish. It is unutterable, the horror and disgust with which I [Coverdale] listened, and saw that, if these things were to be believed, the individual soul was virtually annihilated, and all that is sweet and pure in our present life debased, and that the idea of man's eternal responsibility was made ridiculous, and immortality rendered, at once, impossible, and not worth acceptance. But I would have perished on the spot, sooner than believe it.[6]

Thus does Hawthorne react to what Twain many times described as the confidence man's ability to "work" his audience with mechanical efficiency and hidden contempt. But at the end Coverdale opts to reject Westervelt as a fraud whose powers are merely simulated.

And yet Coverdale is himself a compromised character judged harshly by Zenobia, and almost as harshly by himself, as a man who does not participate in life but only uses it as material for his imagination. Does it matter that this form of speculation is of the mind rather than of the pocketbook? In *The Blithedale Romance* the confidence man succeeds because people are easily persuaded to yield up the management of their souls. Only the stronger individuals realize that this amounts to a surrender of

6. *The Blithedale Romance*, p. 198.

moral responsibility. Coverdale, though emotionally weak-willed, is intellectually stringent with himself, consciously aware and afraid of the dead isolation of an uninhabited heart. He recognizes in Westervelt the man of no conscience, the man who has already cut himself off from others and who merely uses and then discards the people he meets. Thus Coverdale, the amateur ballad-maker, comes to realize that Westervelt, the professional stage-manager, is a distorted reflection of himself, a ghastly warning of what coldness of the heart may lead to. But, says Coverdale, he prefers not to believe in such possibilities. In the end Hawthorne uses the ambivalent relationship between Westervelt (the spurious showman) and Coverdale (the diffident writer) to explore the theme of artistic creation as an irreverent imitation of divine creation and hence a travesty of life. Morbidly considered, the romance writer is a confidence man every time he comes before the public with a mock-up of experience and asks that it be taken as "real." Hawthorne himself feared that as a writer he was not serving the world as straightforwardly as, let us say, a ship's captain. He "would have perished on the spot sooner than believe it," but perhaps his inability to resist the implication has something to do with what some critics have called his artistic death.[7]

In *The Undiscovered Country* Howells also uses the phenomena of spiritualism to dramatize a personal wavering of conviction—but in a religious rather than an artistic context. Howells does not question the value of the literary activity he is pursuing, any more than Hawthorne doubted the existence of a God and a viable religion based on that assumption; on the other hand, Howells does, throughout his creative life, doubt the extent to which religion can survive a laboratory test and prove itself capable of satisfying the natural human longing for a justified existence. Suffering with a private indecision he called "hope-in-doubt," he reworks Hawthorne's drama. The cruder elements of fraud he leaves to such minor characters as Mrs. Le Roy; to Boynton he gives the monomania of a Hollingsworth, the frigid dutifulness of a Coverdale, and the naive good faith of an excited child. The pale Priscilla becomes the somewhat more

7. See Rudolph R. Von Abele, *The Death of the Artist; A Study of Hawthorne's Disintegration* (The Hague: Nijhoff, 1955).

substantial Egeria, and both girls share the status of innocent victims who petulantly rebel against being more and therefore less than ordinary young women. Both quicken under the care of a friendly, socialistic community. Both thrive on contact with pure air, new milk, and young flowers. Coverdale reemerges to some extent in the bachelor Ford, the rational skeptic who is yet warm-blooded enough to win the affections of a girl starved for life. Indeed, the similarities between *The Blithedale Romance* and *The Undiscovered Country* are fairly obvious, but in the end they emphasize the very important differences.

In the first place, the Boynton-Egeria relationship is only superficially like that of Westervelt and Priscilla. Boynton is the father of the girl he exhibits, and it is only his absorption in the experiments he is performing that subjects him to temporary lapses of the heart. He is troubled with no thought of the harm he is doing by subordinating his daughter's individuality to his own research. He is not a Rappaccini, though his sin is in the same category. Like that savant, Boynton is passionately sincere in hoping to extend man's knowledge beyond the limits of natural phenomena. But his motives are humane in intention, if cruel in effect. Because Boynton is well-meaning, it is possible for Ford and him to achieve in the end a mutual tolerance and frankness which could never have existed between Coverdale and Westervelt. Thus, granted his naiveté, granted his sincerity, is there any sense in which Boynton may be bracketed with Westervelt as a confidence man? Obviously, not without doing violence to his good intentions. His motives and his ends are utterly mistaken, but he is more pitiably deluded than his most credulous victim.

Yet, Boynton is willing to accept the techniques and benefit from the aura of the professional swindler. To Ford, Boynton admits: "I know, as well as you do, that this is a street inhabited by fortune-tellers and charlatans of low degree. For that very reason I have taken our lodgings here. The element, the atmosphere, of simple, unquestioning faith brought into this vicinity by the dupes of these people is, unknown to them, of the highest use, the most vital advantage, to us in our present attempt."[8] In

8. W. D. Howells, *The Undiscovered Country* (Boston: Houghton Mifflin Company, 1880), p. 7.

his own eagerness to believe, he tolerates fraud, and indeed cannot always distinguish between what he wants others to believe by any means and what he himself believes by "legitimate" means. Spiritualism, he feels, is an end that justifies the deploying of such material resources as wires, pulleys, and trapdoors. Eventually, of course, he is to recognize what Westervelt had taken for granted from the first—that spiritualism is itself a disguised form of materialism, and that it tends to corrode rather than strengthen the moral fiber of those who believe in it. Boynton is forced to confess that "it is . . . not spiritualism at all, but materialism—a grosser materialism than that which denies; a materialism that asserts and affirms, and appeals for proof to purely physical phenomena. . . . If it has had any effect upon morals, it has been to corrupt them."[9]

In the course of their activities both Westervelt and Boynton prey upon the ignorant emotionalism of their audiences. In *Egeria*, Boynton takes advantage of the innocence of an underdeveloped intelligence and the weakness of an overdeveloped filial piety. For Howells, the realist, such distortions of the norms of experience have to be detrimental to human character, purpose, and accomplishment. No less than Pope, Howells believes that the proper study of mankind is man. But far more systematically he believes that the highest duties of the human being are humane. Thus they are necessarily temporal and terrestrial, worthy only insofar as they produce or promote a social good. Any man who asks for belief in a supernatural world at the expense of an injury to the natural one is abusing the confidence he receives.

If both Westervelt and Boynton are guilty of denaturing the girls they control, so, too, is Selah Tarrant in the beginning of *The Bostonians*. In the "mesmeric-healer," James has created a character with Westervelt's insincerity and repellent good looks and has placed him in Boynton's position as the father of an unusually innocent and responsive young girl. Hawthorne's mesmerist had been a version of the Devil archetype; Howells's had been a specimen of an aberrant type of religious fanatic. James, however, is more interested in class distinctions and less interested in affiliations that are not immediately translatable into

9. Ibid., pp. 366–67.

decisions of social decorum. Thus Tarrant is first and foremost
described as belonging to a socially obnoxious category of men:
"Ransom simply loathed him, from the moment he opened his
mouth; he was intensely familiar—that is, his type was; he was
simply the detested carpetbagger. He was false, cunning, vulgar,
ignoble; the cheapest kind of human product."[10] Like other
confidence men we have seen, he is represented as having a fluent
tongue and expressive hands. His "cures" are effected by the
persuasions of this tongue and these hands, and his daughter
simply provides him with a more musical voice and a more
charming body through which to work his spurious effects.
Again, like most other confidence men he is "a moralist without
a moral sense," and only his daughter's absolute innocence prevents her from being something worse—an immoral accomplice.

Tarrant plays a small part in the book, for Olive Chancellor
quite soon and quite literally "buys him off" in order to take his
place as Verena's mentor. In this exchange the petty charlatan
is replaced by the morally complex and passionately sincere
young woman, an enlightened Bostonian who would never have
been interested in the Veiled Lady. And Verena *is* different.
Though of a yielding nature like Priscilla, she has positive qualities—warm coloring, musical voice, lively mind, and pleasing
manners which make one think rather of Zenobia. Passive
though she may be, she is too richly endowed to remain the
property of a man like her father. Tarrant is present and opera-
tive only briefly as the background from which Olive "rescues"
her protégée.

In these three books by Hawthorne, Howells, and James, we
find the confidence man as mesmerist and stage-manager in the
context of New England reform and the convulsions of social
experiment. In *The Blithedale Romance* the utopian scheme of
communal life on the farm is seen from the start as a somewhat
frivolous adventure engaged in for the most part by people
whose natural growth in the world has been stunted or deformed,
and whose hopes of regenerating society are therefore more
ironic than quixotic. In such a context the confidence man
(Westervelt) is the extreme example of the detached man who

10. Henry James, *The Bostonians* (New York: The Modern Library,
1956), p. 58.

would refashion other lives without having attained fully human status himself.

In *The Undiscovered Country* the community of the Shakers becomes a refuge for Boynton and his daughter; the pastoral setting and earnest hopes of the "Family" are treated with a tolerance and kindliness that condemns only at last and with regret. In this context the confidence man (Boynton) is the man who takes his hopes most seriously. He plays false with life not by trying to change it but by trying to circumvent it. Howells's tone is characteristically mild, but he makes it clear that Boynton's error is the unhealthy aggravation of a longing everyone shares.

By contrast, Selah Tarrant, like all the other characters of *The Bostonians*, belongs to a society made up of distorted personalities, tested and evaluated not in relation to a healthy norm but in relation to each other. Everyone is abnormal; hence, the confidence man, whose peculiar faculty is to exploit the norm, can be of little help to the social satirist. And where personal passion is inextricably allied with a point of view, a theoretical stance, the confidence man cannot retain his power—for he almost never has convictions of his own. Thus his interest must necessarily be bought out by the bigger passion as well as by the heavier purse. He is simply present in order to be once and for all discounted. Yet he lingers in the background to remind us that Olive is in fact working with the abandoned materials of the con man, and that her "truth" is therefore never too far removed from his quackery. What could reflect more harshly on the Boston of these Bostonians?

Had Tarrant kept his control of Verena, he could have wished for no other event than the lecture-hall debut that Olive arranges. The difference in crude terms is that he would have known just exactly what the audience was paying for. He would have realized that the craving for sensation, for aesthetic stimulation and emotional release, was equally present and interwoven with the desire for moral guidance and spiritual leadership.

In *The Leatherwood God* (1916), Howells develops this theme even further. He shows us people willing to believe that an Ohio valley can become a New Jerusalem where perfect harmony reigns. Instead, what happens is that a father and daughter turn their faces from each other, a man and a wife are forcibly separated, and a peaceful community is riven apart and aligned into factions that grow increasingly bitter, intolerant, and violent. The agent of this social disruption is a stranger who first reveals himself to Leatherwood at an ordinary camp meeting. By Howells's standards, such a man would have to be a moral monster. By his own later announcement, the man is Jehovah incarnate, the Lord God Himself. Only a Melville would let such an equation stand. Howells soon shows us that we are dealing in fact only with Joseph Dylks, a robust and good-looking ne'er-do-well who has discovered that in rural Ohio credulity is almost infinitely elastic. In another time and place Dylks had married a girl, Nancy, who had come from a well-to-do Leatherwood family. Subsequently he had deserted her and left her to believe that he was dead, that she was free to return to Leatherwood and marry again. His sudden appearance there is as much of a private anguish for her as it is a tantalizing mystery to the local farmers. They have never seen anyone like him before. Certain physical peculiarities add to his quality as a phenomenon: he wears his hair in a long, thick mane and has a bronchial condition that makes him capable of a loud and equine snort. As it happens, he is among people who cannot clearly distinguish between the bizarre and the divine. They are quite ready to believe that Brother Dylks is an inspired prophet; they are even more willing to believe that he is *the* prophet expected as a new Messiah; and finally, some are little short of eager to believe that he is God Himself. Surely few confidence men ever claimed so much, or ever were, for a time, so successful.

As explained in a prefatory note to the book, Howells based the story of Dylks on the actual events recorded by Judge Taneyhill in the *Ohio Valley Historical Series* (1870). Van Wyck Brooks also tells us that the story was probably told to young Howells and that some of the families affected by the events were actually known to him.[11] Despite the frank use of certain passages from Taneyhill's narrative, Howells as frankly invented incident and character. Actually the studied dialect, homely atmosphere, and thick-soled, plodding action of the first chapter

11. Van Wyck Brooks, *Howells, His Life and World* (New York: E. P. Dutton & Co., 1959), p. 3.

remind one rather more of George Eliot in her *Adam Bede* phase than of the other, sprightlier novel about religion in Ohio, *The Circuit Rider* (1903) by Edward Eggleston. Yet both Howells and Eggleston deal with the peculiarly American form of "revival" enthusiasm. In his one historical novel, Howells describes the false prophet as a consummate confidence man in order to discuss once again the relationship between religious longing and social responsibility.

As we have seen so often, the special advantages or skills of the confidence man provide the best index to the weaknesses of the minds he dominates. Dylks's physical peculiarities have already been noted. We must also see that the popular fascination with his equine traits, while suggesting a quite primitive, almost totemic response, is unreasonable and self-defeating.

It is really as destructive as the sexual attraction which induced Nancy to marry him and which now contributes to the infatuated idolatry of her young niece, Jane. Among the characteristics that impress the men as well as the women is a stentorian voice well adapted to the requirements of a camp-meeting harangue. Dylks is also a master of the appropriate rhetoric for the occasion. He knows how to spellbind with chanted rhythms, electrify with shouts, and quote Scripture with the purpose of a devil, but the memory of an angel. As Howells specifically tells us, Dylks brings forth sighs of contentment from women who know the Bible by heart. When he is encouraged by moans from the younger women and battle cries from the men, he is again proving himself perfectly equipped for his experiment. In fact Squire Braile compliments him by asserting that he has all but one or two of the prerequisites for a worldwide imposture.

Yet he fails. The main reason Squire Braile gives is that Dylks lacks the courage to act his part with conviction when his position is threatened. One might also say that he lacks the higher form of intelligence which would have been capable of organizing and directing the passions set free by his words. Or one might say that he lacks ultimate confidence in himself, without which a con man is an Antaeus with his feet off the ground. He does come to feel the effects of his own power and to half believe in the wild claims he makes. But this is very different from believing in himself—that is to say, in his capacity for inventing the terms of his imposture and then living up to them. That would be strength of a kind, whereas his actual tendency to take himself seriously is a weakness that puts him closer to the level—and eventually in the power—of the people he has deceived. Squire Braile's condemnation is based on Dylks's failure of consistency, and yet this old man, the town "infidel," recognizes that the difference between Dylks and more famous prophets is one of degree and quality, rather than of kind:

It must have been so with all the imposters in the world, from Mahomet up and down! Why, there isn't a false prophet in the Old Testament that couldn't match experiences with you! That's the way it's always gone: first the liar tells his lie, and some of the fools believe it, and proselyte the other fools, and when there are enough of them, their faith begins to work on the liar's own unbelief, till he takes his lie for the truth. Was that the way, you miserable skunk? [12]

The tone and diction here are almost Twain-like. But the full scope of Howells's criticism is not apparent until Dylks clearly states what we have seen all along: "You think I had to lie to them, to deceive them, to bewitch them. . . . They did the lying and deceiving and bewitching themselves. . . ." [13] The victims con themselves. Thus, in what has become a classic pattern, the confidence man becomes the author's agent for the purposes of social criticism.

Yet Howells is not interested in supernally evil characters, any more than in impossibly good ones. Dylks is no Westervelt. Rather, he is a weak, unhappy man who admits that he has himself known the longing he takes advantage of in other men. He has instinctively felt that everyone wishes to "touch a god in the flesh," and in a perverse way, his masquerade is a pageant honoring that need and attempting to satisfy it. At this point we may feel disposed to pardon Dylks. His outrageous hoax at least shows the qualities of audacity, simplicity, and (coeval with the mercenary motive) an impulse that is a debased but recognizable hunger of the spirit. But Howells, with the overwhelming logic of small realities, forces us to see clearly. He makes it obvious

12. W. D. Howells, *The Leatherwood God* (New York: The Century Co., 1916), p. 173.
13. Ibid.

that any man claiming the power to substitute another world for this one is necessarily and unforgivably weakening social responsibility. Such a man is making all men unworthy of a better existence, either here or anywhere else. Of course the confidence man is only a temporary threat in a world where there are women like Nancy, earnestly moral, quick to suffer, but quick to pity—or men like Squire Braile, sanely skeptical, but wisely kind. Between "the laws of Ohio" and the promptings of two charitable hearts, Joseph Dylks is, if not quite reformed, at least rendered harmless to all but himself.

In making the confidence man claim to be a god, Howells takes him to the edge of a kind of psychological displacement that seems closer to a disease of the mind than a professional ploy. But Dylks remains craven rather than "cracked," too human to prove more than the necessity of judging people as men first and spirits afterward. He demonstrates Howells's conviction that people are less than human if they try to be more.

Howells's friend Mark Twain also had something to contribute to the literature of fake spiritualists. As might be expected, he brings with him a Western familiarity with prodigies and a humorous respect for the author of *The Humbugs of the World*. From the point of view of Twain and the great humbug authority P. T. Barnum, the spiritual claimant was a brazen opportunist. If we recall Twain's own experiences with the mesmerist described in the *Autobiography* (and discussed in Chapter Three), we can see that he knew the possibilities of the role from having tested them himself. He knew how easy it was to persuade an audience to believe in its own excitement. Those who succumbed to the hysteria of spiritualism no doubt appeared to him as only a mutant form of the species "human fool." Like a sharper fang or a keener nose, the spiritual "line" was developed by certain con men as a predatory advantage.

In *Innocents Abroad* Twain describes priestcraft as an archetypal form of humbuggery, but is moved to greater indignation by the Jaffa colony of American enthusiasts under the leadership of the prophet Adams. The enterprise dissolved under the pressures of famine and disease, and Twain describes the case with his frequent mixture of humorous awe and real indignation. He is astonished by the audacity of the con man and the naive stupidity of his dupes: "The colony [a kind of visionary Utopia] was a complete *fiasco*. . . . The prophet Adams—once an actor, then several other things, afterward a Mormon and a missionary, always an adventurer—remains at Jaffa with his handful of sorrowful subjects."[14]

Twain was openly satirical in his description of a less harmful and less ambitious drain on the spiritual hopes of his contemporaries. In *Life on the Mississippi* he describes a medium named Manchester. Like Barnum's J. V. Mansfield[15] (on whom Twain's character may be based), Manchester invites the public to address him with questions to be asked of the dead spirits; if the postage is prepaid, the answers will be sent by return mail. Twain's attitude is clear as he explains the rates: "From the local post-office in Paradise to New York, five dollars; from New York to St. Louis, three cents."[16] He tells of his own visit to Manchester, of his desire to speak, through him, to the spirit of a friend's dead uncle. The ensuing dialogue humorously reveals the boredom of a heaven where no one eats, drinks, smokes, or reads a book. But the uncle's spirit seems to have difficulty in handling the sort of specific question which Manchester could not know how to answer; the medium's outrageously inaccurate guesses in these cases leave the fraud totally exposed. Yet it is shown to have a nearly profound quality in the simplicity with which it preys on man's eagerness to accept any offer of contact with an external source of strength and wisdom. Twain's humor has a light touch here; it does not flay, but it does undress a human weakness and show us the homely, somewhat funny, and embarrassingly familiar sight of its nakedness.

In *Following the Equator,* Twain mentions the "Benares god," who is a man accepted and treated like a divine personage in a way that reminds us of Taji among the Mardians. This man-god illustrates a religious phenomenon which would seem to be peculiar to India. Actually it is only another case of a man playing a part he knows his audience would rather believe in than

14. Twain, *Innocents Abroad*, 2: 398–400.
15. P. T. Barnum, *The Humbugs of the World* (New York: Carleton Publisher, 1866), p. 85.
16. Twain, *Life on the Mississippi*, p. 386.

not, for reasons of their own. The showman in Twain recognizes the style of a professional performance, and characteristically notes its commercial value: "If Barnum—but Barnum's ambitions are at rest. This god will remain in the holy peace and seclusion of his garden, undisturbed. Barnum could not have gotten him, anyway. Still, he would have found a substitute that would answer." [17] Twain did of course create his own version of a divine visitant in *The Mysterious Stranger*. Philip Traum is not only a supernatural being, but himself a magician who turns the whole world into a sideshow. Twain can deal with the spiritual claimant seriously only after he has himself gone beyond satire to a complete rejection of the real world. He succumbs, if only temporarily, to a complete loss of faith in the durability of human dignity, its strength to survive the exposure of human error and weakness. Philip Traum is not an opportunist, not a confidence man, even though he abuses the confidence of his young friends in Eseldorf. He is what he claims to be. The trust he might have betrayed, the hope he might have bejuggled, the fear and despair he might have fed upon—these are no more substantial than he is. The real confidence man who claims supernatural attributes presupposes for his field of operations a natural world with very mundane attributes. Such a world is the setting for Twain's best work. There, as we have already seen in Chapter Three, the artist in Twain fully appreciates and recognizes a kindred (if demonic) spirit in the confidence man.

In review, then, it seems that the proliferation of divinely inspired human beings suggests not that heaven had condescended to grant more privileges, but that more applicants were feeling themselves entitled to favors. The rudimentary impulse of the democratic spirit seems to have been "Why not me?" and where there was sufficient piety—or rascality—the answer seems to have been more and more often, "Why not, indeed!" But although it may be easy to convince oneself, how turn others into devout disciples, or unconscious dupes? The method appears to have been frighteningly simple. One had only to take advantage of a habit of superstition and a love of prodigies. One had only to play upon the latent belief in progress, in the feeling that a

17. Twain, *Following the Equator*, 2: 214.

people clever enough to join two oceans would soon be able to join two worlds. Finally, one had only to feed the craving for aesthetic stimulation, so rarely satisfied on the frontier.

The crudest appeal to the imagination would stir the emotions, rouse interest in the unknown, and awaken the senses to the special endowments of rare individuals—the ethereal delicacy of a girl like Priscilla Moodie or the animal magnetism of a man like Joseph Dylks. The display of personality, the element of theatricality, is almost universally apparent here, and helps to explain the peculiar interest taken in these con men by Hawthorne, Howells, and Twain.

Indeed one of the distinguishing marks of these confidence men is their charismatic quality, their success as the focal point of crowd interest and even of crowd hysteria. Nearly all the confidence men appearing in this chapter are physically attractive; they use as their "weapon" the communicative organs, the burning eye and the thrilling tongue. Their "skill" is in the mastery of religious jargon, and their "game" is the manipulation of a primitive soul hunger. It is a hunger which feeds not only on crude representations of the spiritual life, but also on those flamboyant and magnetic personalities which contrast so strongly with the ordinary man's inhibited or less colorful self. The influence of the spiritual claimant is yet another result of the visionary habit induced by the rapidly expanding boundaries of every kind of enterprise. And insofar as this naiveté is innocent, the confidence man appears as the Snake in "God's country."

CHAPTER FIVE

To the Old World

American innocence is generally considered to be the domain of Henry James. Certainly here we might expect some fine and complex handling of the confidence man, and indeed that is the case. In approaching James from the direction we have come, we should note that at the same time that the West could still be called "new," there were people for whom the actual process of getting a living out of the land was relegated to the past tense or perhaps a dead ancestor, or in the case of many women, an absentee husband. Primary attention was now to be given to the uses of money, to enjoying its translation into comfort, cultivation, and the power of selection. In his own forty-two-year history, James's Christopher Newman passes through the phase of money-making to arrive at the phase of money-using, coincident, as he expresses it, with the "longing for a new world." For him as for many others, the unknown continent is Europe. With its old cities, old art, old names, and old prejudices, it is, as James often points out, a new opportunity for the spirit of enterprise and the attitude of appropriation. Geographically, we have come a long way from Shirley's Indian Bar mines, but socially and culturally it is still a question of "staking a claim," and of being sometimes defrauded.

The theme of Mark Twain's *American Claimant* registers the cruder type of "Europhilia," the romantic infatuation with those degrees and distinctions and courtesies which show as graces now that they have ceased, since the Revolution, to be felt as oppressions. To get the benefit of them without the penalty was a not uncommon American dream. In speaking of the American ap-

proach to Europe, Kenneth Lynn makes a significant transition
from Mark Twain to Henry James using the theme of the confidence man: "Translating the comedy of the confidence game
from a frontier locale to the great stage of Europe, and viewing
the comedy not from an amused outsider's standpoint, but from
the potential victim's, Twain [in *Innocents Abroad*] wrote the
first act of an international drama that would be Henry James's
greatest theme" (Lynn, pp. 155–56). Henry James, Sr., already
shows an appreciation of what could be bought on the European
market—for example, a "better sensuous education than they
[his sons] are likely to get here."[1] In short, that awakening of
the American imagination described in the first three chapters
as primarily a response to the natural resources of the land becomes now a response to the cultural resources of the past. His-
torically speaking, every American had left some of his belong-
ings in Europe. It was now convenient for him to reclaim them.
But having been away for three hundred years, he found that it
took some effort to get his bearings and some experience to tell
the friend from the pickpocket. In the writing of Henry James,
the American in Europe is often in some sense "taken in" or deceived; in a few cases the European (or Europeanized American)
acts the part of a confidence man in relation to the "innocent"
American.

But what, indeed, is the "innocent American"? Probably no
one writing of James can resist the temptation to define for his
own benefit what James meant by that phrase. It should not
be surprising that a concept rich enough to pay for almost a lifetime of literary analysis should be, by the same token, rich
enough to support a good many small definitions. For our own
purposes it is worth noting that the American most easily duped
is the American who brings with him more of his country than he
leaves behind. His innocence is really the consummate assurance
with which he brings his moral geography with him, as though he
expects to navigate London by a map of New York. What happens, of course, is that he misses connections, is obtuse, really,
in his failure to recognize the degree of intimacy, of collusion,
of intersecting lines and obstructions in the relationships around

1. Henry Seidel Canby, *Turn West, Turn East: Mark Twain and Henry
James* (Boston, 1951), p. 47.

him. He sees, it may be, the avenues, but not the byways which carry the more significant traffic. Insofar as American terrain is less cultivated, is freer, wider, more prominently spacious, it offers so much less experience with tortuous deceit, with involute evil. Thus, when he is led by the hand, the American in Europe is at the mercy of his guide.

How costly this dependence can be is shown most directly by Caroline Spencer, the heroine of *Four Meetings* (1877). Her guides mislead her long before she sets foot in another country, for they can easily be consulted at home; they are the decorative travelogues and pretty romances to be found in the subscription library, the eloquent photographs and refurbished memories of travelers who have come back from abroad—to all of which she gives herself avidly and with the clinging intelligence of a maiden schoolteacher. She meets the narrator at a party in the small New England town where she lives and soon discovers that he is something of an expatriate. Her tenacity in drawing upon his fund of European experience is so unusually sincere that he tells her she has "the native American passion—the passion for the picturesque."[2] She confides that she is saving her money for the sole purpose of going abroad. As soon as she has the necessary amount, she plans to make Europe briefly her own.

The second of the four meetings takes place several years later in the port of le Havre. Caroline Spencer has just arrived to begin her long-planned adventure, and the narrator has come there to meet visiting relatives. Discovering her seated alone in a small café, he reopens their acquaintance and congratulates her on having at last taken up her option. Her delight is already intense, although she has yet only a foothold on the immense satisfaction she promises herself. The narrator soon learns that she has been met by a cousin, a struggling art student from Paris. Although the narrator is surprised to hear of him, it appears that Miss Spencer happily considers him a piece of that "dear old Europe" she has come to see. After all, even in provincial New England she has heard that art students are often poor, but that they are dedicated followers of an ideal; that they are usually loved by great women whose families object; and that they

2. Henry James, *The Complete Tales of Henry James*, ed. Leon Edel (Philadelphia and New York: J. B. Lippincott Co., 1962), 4: 92.

inevitably produce a masterpiece that brings fame, fortune, and forgiveness tumbling down on their heads like an avalanche. Content in this belief, she seems to have been much taken with her cousin. She has even allowed him to take charge of her accumulated funds to see them safely to the bank. Upon hearing this, the narrator is unpleasantly startled by the thought that she has been "taken," indeed.

The third meeting confirms his worst suspicions. He finds her now at her inn, temporarily alone and obviously distressed. He has already met the cousin, who seems to his educated eye a vulgar opportunist, with no fine sensibilities either aesthetic or moral. It is therefore with growing outrage that he listens to Miss Spencer's story. She has been appealed to by her cousin. He is, she explains quite pathetically, a man of great talent but insufferably poor. Quite wonderfully, he has had the great good fortune (though not, alas, in a monetary sense) to love and be loved by a lady of noble birth. Her family—and what monsters it proves them!—objected most strenuously to a marriage. But she—magnificently—has testified to her love by giving her hand. Fastly married, conclusively poor, they must wait until the "great Picture" arrives to save them. Meanwhile, of course, they must eat.

By this time, the narrator has grasped the situation in all its ugly detail and sees that the "cousin" may or may not be a first-rate painter, but is certainly an accomplished "con artist." His tongue may chatter about "nice bit[s] of color," and quaint genre scenes, but its true relish is for the plump apricots he has for his dinner. He is the worst sort of materialist, painting over his greed with the colors of the gaudiest romance. Yet when he appeals to Caroline for her money, she quietly, firmly, confidently turns over to him all of her savings, leaving herself only the fare for the next boat to America.

The last of the four meetings takes place again in New England. Passing through North Verona years later, the narrator recalls Miss Spencer and decides to pay her a visit. He discovers that she has never returned to Europe—but—Europe has returned to her, in the very palpable form of her cousin's French wife. She is in fact his widow, and since he died before his great picture was vouchsafed him, she is still penniless. To whom should she turn but to the New England lady whose understanding had already been proven, though perhaps not repaid? When he meets the Provençal "Countess," the narrator at once sees her to be of the commonest Parisian clay, possibly of the landlady mold, and remarkable only for the audacity with which she has imposed herself on the schoolteacher's life—and salary. He is deeply shocked by this confidence game, but senses that Caroline half knows and half shrinks from knowing the full extent to which her trust has been shamefully abused. In leaving her for the last time, the narrator remarks to himself that she has, indeed, been given a share of Europe—not of its beauties and refinements, but of what Howells once called "the veteran duplicities of that continent."

In *Four Meetings*, Caroline's cousin and his wife represent the actual sordidness and rapacity which is a part of European life, but which is left out of the glamorized picture that Americans believe in. Their power, like that of the other confidence men we have seen, comes from their detached but thorough knowledge of other people's illusions. They do not mind playing the parts that Americans have created for them. After all, the native has always the moral advantage over the tourist. In one way or another the visitor must pay the price of admission and abide the performance. Caroline's special fate is to have paid so high for an act so cheap. One reason for this may be that, as a true daughter of New England, she has had too little experience with the comedy of life. The "context-story" of "fallen grandeur," which, as we have seen in Twain's King and Duke, is the best excuse for self-pity (and a lack of funds), provides for Caroline the rudiments of a "cause." She responds with an inherited alacrity to the demand for sacrifice, clearly preferring it to the opportunity for pleasure. In short, the topography of her mind —the earnest sympathies for hardship, for kin, for cultural endeavor—gives her no clue to "the lay of the land" in "Old Europe." She is individually and typically innocent. Finally, we may say that her great hopes and her great illusions, her morbid little strength and her colossal futility are all revealed to us by the confidence man.

But Caroline Spencer is a very weak specimen of what, in James's hands, the American girl may become. In *The Portrait of a Lady* (1880) and in *The Wings of the Dove* (1902), we are dealing with two young women whose illusions are consistent with the idea of their intelligence, because the "performances" they attend are brilliantly conceived and exquisitely cast. Madame Merle and Kate Croy, in spite of their great difference, are both extraordinarily well-finished products of a highly organized society, one in which marriage is an alliance rather than a partnership, and in which intrigue is the natural recourse for those interested in securing "good terms" for their side. In such a context it is not surprising that the confidence woman plays the role of a matchmaker who falsifies her client's position.

Serena Merle is an American by birth and a Swiss by marriage, but she is so thoroughly Europeanized, so prominently cosmopolitan, so inveterately widowed, that she comes as near as a person may to representing the methods of social existence apart from the accrued benefits, the local rewards and personal satisfactions of living. Isabel at first thinks that Madame Merle does not have a private life at all, but exists solely through her connection with myriads of unrelated people. It is Madame Merle's perfect understanding of what these people want and expect from each other that gives her an extra cunning and a specialized skill, which are the assets of the confidence man. The arts of social entertainment are her "weapons," and it can be said, as Isabel also comes to realize, that her charm is as "professional" as a doctor's kind touch.

Yet, despite the fact that she lives off the hospitality of those whom she keeps in ignorance of her past, she is not for this reason a confidence woman in any usable sense. Her contributions to any drawingroom activity are genuine enough and deserve to be genuinely appreciated. She becomes a confidence woman only after hearing of Isabel's inheritance and only when she schemes to get the benefit of that money. Her plan is of course to marry Isabel to the father of her own illegitimate child. By this means she hopes to provide her daughter with the chance to make the kind of brilliant marriage she herself could never attain. The fact that Madame Merle is a disappointed woman acting out of despair gives her the sort of moral and emotional complexity that we should expect in a Jamesian character. Madame Merle is not crudely selfish. She does, indeed, think of Pansy as a reincarnation of herself, but her affection for the girl is as real as it is subterranean, and for this reason it is an excuse as well as an incentive for intrigue.

Her "game" works because she has a powerful ally in Gilbert Osmond and because Isabel's type of American innocence makes her an almost too easy victim. Fitted out with every advantage that nature and her cousin Ralph can bestow, Isabel is as eager as any Western pioneer to find her "opportunity" for investment. And, like Caroline Spenser (though in a far more refined way), she is ready to see nobility and romance in the person of an artist too sensitive to be grossly well off. At this point Osmond becomes Madame Merle's tool, ordered by her to perform in a certain way without bothering himself to question or even to understand the larger objectives. With Isabel's marriage to Osmond, the "game" ends.

Success, however, is conditional. Her own limitations prevent Madame Merle from seeing beyond the social fact of the marriage to the moral fact of Isabel's commitment to principle. Despite cruel pressure, Isabel will not "use" Pansy's heart or Lord Warburton's trust. In the end she triumphs over Madame Merle by learning of her deep treachery and pitying her for the unhappiness that led to it. Yet when Isabel remarks that Madame Merle has set sail with the new purpose of "making a convenience of America," she unconsciously hints that this lady belongs to the category of itinerant and indestructible con men.

In *The Wings of the Dove* James creates a character who, like Madame Merle, plots the marriage of the man who is her most intimate friend to the woman who is her most wealthy acquaintance. But whereas Madame Merle is a tired expatriate, hoping to salvage a compensation for the failure of her own ambitions, Kate is a young, energetic, bountifully optimistic girl who is trying to build her future on the best foundation available. In this respect she is more like Isabel than like Madame Merle, except that for Kate "foundation" means a bankbook, while for Isabel it means a theory. Nevertheless Kate is fresh and engaging; the world is before, not behind, her, and her capacity to feel passionately and to think brilliantly is part of a rich characterization in the forefront of the novel. Her prominence and complexity entitle her to a more thorough study than Madame Merle requires.

Kate, to begin with, requires not only to subsist, but to live up to the full potential of her natural endowments. These are fine health, great beauty, rare intelligence, and the poise that comes from a full knowledge of how well these qualities complement each other. In demanding that her life make full use of what she brings to it, she recognizes only two alternative courses of action: one is that she shall renounce all hopes of wealth and love in a comprehensive gesture of loyalty to her outcast father, and the other is that she shall discard him entirely and accept no less than everything that wealth and love have to offer. In the first chapter Lionel Croy makes it clear that he does not want *her*, but only what she can do for him if she marries well. By his rejection of her offer to live with him, as well as by the sordid history he bequeathes to her, he impels, one might say he pushes, her into a commitment to her other alternative. Thus, to the achievement of love enjoyed in luxury (and hence to her role as confidence woman), Kate brings all the intellectual and emotional control which would have sustained her had she been allowed to make her grand sacrifice. As it is, she devotes all of her capacities, all of her self-discipline, to the task of avoiding all sacrifice. She uses her wit to plan for her love, and her sex to win the last argument. It is true, as Densher admiringly recognizes, that "her passion and her intelligence [are] one." Out of this union she conceives her "game." First she plans to keep her engagement a secret from Aunt Maud and then, when the opportunity suggests it, to arrange for Densher to court a dying girl for her money.

It is at this point that we must note the degree to which the conditions of her society dictate the ends and means of her "game." Like many confidence men, and like Madame Merle in particular, Kate for all practical purposes accepts the morality of her society far more consistently and truthfully than most of its other members. She faces the fact that in the society to which she has been elevated by Aunt Maud and committed by her father, the good life is the moneyed one. Her eyes are open. She sees that good taste is an expensive habit and that good manners correspond to the absence of financial worries. Under these circumstances, good behavior is demonstrable only through the uses of money, and it fails to register unless the sums are large. Kate sees in Densher the fineness of intellection and appreciation that would create for her endless opportunities to make money a blessing. Thus, without the sanction of wealth, Kate's engagement to Densher is in a sense unregenerate. It lacks the grace of Aunt Maud's fortune, and therefore it can do no good works and has no power to save itself. However much we condemn Kate as mercenary, certainly we must recognize the socially conditioned sense in which she wishes not simply to be good, or even just good enough, but rather as good as she can possibly be. By her lights she is ambitious of heaven. And so, therefore, is Densher, if one considers that Kate's mind and body are his paradise, and that its rules for possession are the laws of his life.

If Kate is aware of the values of London society, she also understands the machinery of its motion. She is taught the rudiments by her sister Marian. This practical woman is quite frank in expecting Kate to turn Mrs. Lowder's interest in her to account: Marian "desired her to 'work' Lancaster Gate as she believed that scene of abundance could be worked."[3] Later, in describing the fortune-hunting Lord Mark to Milly, Kate shows that she now takes the wheels and levers for granted: "[Lord Mark] was working Lancaster Gate for all it was worth: just as it was, no doubt, working *him*, and just as the working and the worked were in London, as one might explain, the parties to every relation" (1:178). Her tone is quite free from the condemnation that would have made her a paltry hypocrite. Instead, she impresses us with the clarity and honesty of her insight. She goes on to explain that "... every one who had anything to give—it was true they were the fewest—made the sharpest possible bargain for it, got at least its value in return ..." (1:179). This, of course, is just what Milly will later refuse to do when Lord Mark asks her to accept him. Her reply will be: "I give and give and give—there you are; ... Only I can't listen or receive or accept—I can't *agree*. I can't make a bargain" (2:161). Yet for those who *can*, like Kate,

3. James, *The Wings of the Dove* (New York: Charles Scribner's Sons, 1902), 1:43. Future references to this edition will be indicated by page numbers in my text.

the machinery has its attractive qualities of intricate fittings, neat joinings, and ground edges, all of which make for a pleasant smoothness of function. As she concludes in her description, "The worker in one connection was the worked in another; it was as broad as it was long—with the wheels of the system, as might be seen, wonderfully oiled. People could quite like each other in the midst of it . . ." (1:179). Kate's plan fits into the mechanism without causing a hitch. Nothing so gross as dirt or stones is introduced, nothing like clatter or din is allowed, nothing is done that would attract the attention of the guardians of institutionalized morality, the policeman or the priest. As Kate says, everyone has a rather nice time through it all. But the point, as Frederick Crews explains, is that "in purifying the motives of his characters James has reached a stage at which personal enmity [and one might add violence] is not only unnecessary to evil-doing, it is regarded as an element of moral redundancy."[4] With the greatest economy, James isolates and refines his conception of evil-doing in *The Wings of the Dove*. It becomes the deadliest effect of nothing worse than a too-consistently applied theory of social manipulation (on Kate's part) and (on Densher's) a too-narrowly conceived opinion of what loyalty to one woman may excuse in deception of another.

James makes it clear that Kate and Densher are exquisite moral organisms. Indeed, it is the richness of what they offer each other that makes them think a high price worth paying. "[They are] a pair of natures well nigh consumed by a sense of their intimate affinity and congruity, the reciprocity of their desire, and thus passionately impatient of barriers and delays, yet with qualities of intelligence and character that they are meanwhile extraordinarily able to draw upon for the enrichment of their relation, the extension of their prospect and the support of their 'game' " (1:xix). The "game" here is of course their agreement to deceive Aunt Maud, but it prefigures their relationship with Milly Theale. The exclusiveness and intensity of their private alliance puts them in opposition to society, although it is Kate's intention that when they "go public," they shall do so on Aunt Maud's terms. Meanwhile, society is simply a means to their end. And

4. Frederick C. Crews, *The Tragedy of Manners* (New Haven: Yale University Press, 1957), p. 59.

therefore they inevitably prejudice themselves against the autonomous rights and desires of any individual member of that society. As James explains in the Preface, ". . . all unconsciously and with the best faith in the world, all by mere force of the terms of their superior passion combined with their superior diplomacy, they are laying a trap for the great innocence to come" (1:xix–xx).

Milly, when she does arrive, offers the perfect contrast to Kate; that is, instead of needing money to enjoy life, she needs life to enjoy money, or rather the options it gives her. In a sense the development of Kate's "plan" is but the increasing assertiveness of Kate's stronger vitality, her greater life expectancy, in every sense of the term. Yet what aids her even more than Milly's illness is Milly's initial loneliness, the craving to be fully and completely understood by a friend stronger and wiser than Susan. Ultimately only Dr. Luke Strett is able to fill this place, but the need is at first so clearly apparent that half of Kate's work is already done for her. It is always the perfection of Milly's need suiting her own provision that Kate delights in. It might be for motives of the purest charity that she lends her lover to someone who needs an interest in life. In truth, however, her pleasure is more like that of an inventor who achieves his solution with an unexpected economy of means. Urging Densher to take up the function she has designed for him, she admits: " 'I verily believe I *shall* hate you if you spoil for me the beauty of what I see!' " (2:30) From such hints as these we gather (as Densher does only too late) that while he is the object and beneficiary of the scheme, he is as much its pawn as Milly herself. When he refuses to go on with the plan unless Kate becomes his mistress, he only partly understands what his victory means. He asks for it as a measure of her love for him, but it actually measures her faith in her scheme.

As a confidence woman she does indeed succeed. She must be content, however, with a technical triumph. She had expected Milly to leave her money to Densher, thinking he was in love with her. What she did not expect was that Milly, at last seeing through the hoax, should still leave the money to him, and thus render the "game" pointless. And if pointless, then despicable. Densher's renunciation of the money, and with it Kate, is often spoken of as his "salvation." But in fact it is not the result of a sudden moral growth. With the legacy representing Milly's knowledge and forgiveness, Densher's acceptance of it would not be qualified by the thought of any real happiness he may have given and which may have been genuinely appreciated and thus honestly rewarded. Without extenuation, he would be feeding and clothing himself at the expense of her death. And though he has been able to degrade himself for love, it has never, as James would say, been open to him to do it for money. He draws the line rather suddenly and Kate finds herself standing on the other side of it, morally condemned for her confidence game.

Milly, as the victim of this game, is far more complicated than Caroline Spencer, and far less aggressive than Isabel. Yet all three stand forth as American women for whom Europe represents an expansion of opportunity, and who happen to represent for "Europe" a timely financial boon. Although, as Mrs. Stringham notes, Milly is "starved for culture," she is abundantly provided with the best and at the same time the most characteristic benefits that America can give—a vaguely buccaneering past resulting in huge chests of gold, the large independence of "a merely personal tradition," and a growing impatience to take on the world. Her "innocence" does in a way consist of her carrying this "New York legend" around with her. She has a manner of not comprehending any difficulty short of death, and she specifies her desire to meet "people" with the liberal sweep of intent that is as democratic as it is regal. In New York Milly had no objections to Densher's social and financial status. She was simply pleased with the man himself. It is on this same basis that she continues to think of him in London and Venice. She sees Kate's "rejection" of him as evidence of a personal antipathy which cannot be remedied. Could she have understood from the beginning the true obstacle to his marriage with Kate, she might have guessed that there were ways in which it could be remedied at someone else's expense. But she sees no reason to doubt the appearance they make with each other and the liking they show for her. Her American good faith leads her to believe in disinterested friendships, and she utterly believes in Densher and Kate. As confidence men, they therefore show us the folly of trusting out of the desire and habit of trust. But though they may isolate for us what is most American in Milly, they can only condemn themselves by the disclosure of what is most bountiful in her—the absolute power to give.

There is a sense, however, in which James distracts our attention from Milly and focuses it on Kate. Not only does he give her the sort of positive vitality that initially attracts Milly, but he also gives her the benefit of sharing his love of design. Both he and she know what it means to construct a plot, to "handle" a snag and "dodge" an obstruction. In his preface to the New York edition of this work, he uses the word "game" to apply to both Kate's subterfuge and his own act of creation. Her tone of private congratulation, her glow of mental exercise are more than matched in the novelist's description of how he contrived her story. This affinity between the "confidence man" character and his author has been noted before. It is not at all unusual for the author's sympathies to be placed with the victim, while his artistic eye follows the villain with an appreciation and affection of its own. Furthermore, it is in the nature of the case that the author should give to the confidence man his most acute perception of the mechanics of society. Of course, as a purely intellectual endowment, it represents, in nineteenth-century parlance, the capacity of the "head," and as such must give way to the "heart." This is what happens when Huck pities the King and the Duke, when Isabel says of Madame Merle, "Ah, poor, poor woman!" and when Milly forgives Merton Densher and Kate. The confidence man fails of his ends because a generous spirit trusts its own instinct. Goodness defeats the sin by pardoning the sinner. But where the author's critical impulse is stronger, as in *Four Meetings*, or where his pessimism works against such an outcome, as in *The Bostonians* (discussed in Chapter Four), then the confidence man keeps his unredeemed status as a debaucher of American innocence.

CHAPTER SIX

And Back to Melville

Leaving the company of Jamesian heroines, we may stop to consider that the vulnerability of their innocence is a far different thing from the weaknesses of most of the victims of the confidence man. Again and again I have stressed the often direct relationship between the success of the con man and the corrupt nature of his victim. Indeed, at the very time that confidence was overflowing in the surveyor's tent and the accounting room, it seems that among writers there was an ebbing of trust in the goodness of man.

During the third quarter of the century, the fair appearance of life in America was suspected of being a thin disguise for the ugly features of an evil society. One very dramatic unmasking of the hidden corruption was the Beecher-Tilton affair; here, one of America's most revered preachers was discovered to be an adulterer. The resulting sense of betrayed confidence is what Kenneth Lynn finds typical of the "mood of the 70s": ". . . a decade in which most Americans wished to believe that everything was fundamentally all right with their society, while at the same time they had a foreboding sense that corrupt forces were at work in it. . . ."[1] As we have ourselves seen in the previous chapters, the greatest writers of the century suffered a loss of confidence which involved to some degree or perhaps temporarily a gain of sensibility. Hawthorne in his austere way distrusted the very art of fiction, but used it as a special glass through which to view the world. The more benign Howells distrusted and inflexibly op-

1. Kenneth S. Lynn, *Mark Twain and Southwestern Humor* (Boston: Little, Brown & Company, 1959), p. 181.

posed a romantic idealism, but shook hands with the realities of ordinary life. What James distrusted may best be called "the uncivilized." Turning from it, he cultivated his acquaintance with the permutations of evil in a highly organized social milieu, putting himself artistically and personally in a company more European than American. Twain, by contrast, was quintessentially American; yet his distrust went at times so far as to include human nature itself, the "damned human race" in a lump. Even so, his is a vehemence that grows out of a correlative desire to trust, a yearning that gives warmth equally to his sentimentality and to his implacable cynicism.

Having recognized that pessimism was the direction in which these men were moving, we should also note the variety of ways in which they used the con man. For they saw in him a perfect means of expressing equivocal attitudes toward their society and toward their own creative activity. Yet only once in the period of this study was the confidence man used to carry the full weight of a piece of fiction, and one might add, the heavy burden of a philosophy widely gathered and deeply meditated. This occasion was, of course, *The Confidence-Man: His Masquerade* (1857). For the purposes of this study, Melville's work has a significance that transcends both chronology and regional affiliation. It therefore seems appropriate to deal with him in the final chapter of this book.

Melville was not really bound to his time or its temper. What may have become for others a "foreboding sense" of corruption in the '70s was for Melville already a strong conviction in the '40s and '50s. Perhaps he stands alone because none of the writers we have discussed (including Hawthorne) suffered quite the emotional privation or the metaphysical hunger of this pedagogue, farmer, and sailor-turned-writer. He, quite simply, distrusted God. That is, he distrusted what the nineteenth-century Christian American meant by that concept. Like Twain, however, he was capable of the naive trust and the bitter disillusionment which are the two manifestations of one longing for the idyllic—the sweeping condemnations being the sort of retaliation that follows a spurned embrace.

But whatever one's feeling about the reliability of one's fellow-man or of one's God, must not a certain confidence exist between a writer and his audience? Does not the creating and the reading of literature involve a relationship of trust? Melville considered the question an important one, and it is possible to trace his feelings about it through the various works preceding *The Confidence-Man*. Because the issue is so vital to an understanding of that book, I shall give here a brief history of Melville's relationship with his reader.

In the preface to *Typee*, he tells us he "[trusts] that his anxious desire to speak the unvarnished truth will gain for him the confidence of his readers."[2] He is a "sailor" speaking to "fireside people" and proposing to give them a corrective account of life on a South Sea island. This does not mean that he does not privately take, and that we do not willingly give, a certain latitude with regard to the "facts." The imaginative truth of all great adventure stories is here faithfully tendered and is received with the pleasurable interest that the book has always commanded. In Melville's second book, *Omoo*, the sailor offers "to give a *familiar* account of the present condition of the converted Polynesians . . . under circumstances most favorable for correct observations on the social conditions of the natives."[3] He claims to be "an unbiased observer," in fact "the most casual observer," unencumbered with prejudice, unequipped with a formula. No such innocence can be claimed for the author of *Mardi*, whose discontented sailor very soon became a self-proclaimed god. In his role as Taji, the sailor (like Ishmael later) puts on the mantle of eternity and lists his reincarnations: "I was at the subsiding of the Deluge . . . I am the leader of the Mohawk [of the Boston Tea Party]. . . . I am the vailed Persian Prophet; I, the man in the iron mask; I, Junius";[4] I, in short, am not what I seem. And so we, at the fireside, are warned that we must not doze in our trust, if we wish to be awake for the truth.

In the next epoch of this history, the reader has been removed

2. Herman Melville, *Typee: A Peep at Polynesian Life* (Evanston, Ill., and Chicago: Northwestern University Press and The Newberry Library, 1968), p. xiv.

3. Herman Melville, *Omoo: A Narrative of Adventures in the South Seas* (Evanston, Ill., and Chicago: Northwestern University Press and The Newberry Library, 1968), pp. xiii–xiv.

4. Herman Melville, *Mardi: and A Voyage Thither* (Evanston, Ill., and Chicago: Northwestern University Press and The Newberry Library, 1970), p. 297.

from the hearth and taken to the schoolroom. In *Redburn* and *White Jacket* Melville gives us a documentary revelation of evils discovered by innocent persons exposed to the world. Redburn is first gently and then, in Liverpool, severely mocked for his child-like illusions. White Jacket is made to lecture on the evils of life in a man-o'-war, which in turn is an explicit microcosm. Despite a few mild ironies, we are asked to believe in the fidelity of the registering mind, the hero's, and in the representativeness of the experience it encounters. We believe in Melville's sincerity, even to the point of wishing it would be less obtrusive.

In *Moby-Dick* and *Pierre*, the author-reader relationship changes to something like that between the dramatist and his audience. We watch as a titanic individual pits himself against the forces that mock his final ignorance and impotence. The rich fabric of the language and dramatic intensity of Ahab in *Moby-Dick* sustain our belief and direct our sympathy. In *Pierre*, however, Melville asks even more of the reader and even goes so far as to suggest a new way of looking at the relationship between an author and his public. Pierre, described as writing a novel under conditions truly diabolical—and perhaps autobiographically tinged—receives the following letter from his publishers: "Sir:—You are a swindler. Upon the pretense of writing a popular novel for us, you have been receiving cash advances from us, while passing through our press the sheets of a blasphemous rhapsody, filched from the vile Atheists, Lucian and Voltaire."[5] Who can doubt that Melville smiled, more or less grimly, as he wrote this?

What follows in the short stories written after *Pierre* suggests that Melville now thought of himself as a kind of secret agent among an alien populace. Dual- and triple-layered masks of character or scene or incident present an innocent face which is in effect a "cover" for a hidden message of despite. The surface story can be taken on trust (as in some cases it was for almost a century) only if the reader is so conditioned as to see no reason for subterfuge. The cycle of gestation in "The Tartarus of Maids," the paranoia in "I and My Chimney," the snubbing of Christianity in "The Lightning Rod Man" are not altogether

5. Herman Melville, *Pierre: or The Ambiguities* (Evanston and Chicago: Northwestern University Press and The Newberry Library, 1971), p. 356.

unlike the camouflaged thumb-to-nose posture of Mark Twain's
Petrified Man. All are gestures of contempt. Melville, in "The
Lightning Rod Man," takes defiant pleasure in the fact that
lightning can flash from the earth back at the sky. John Paul
Jones, in *His Fifty Years of Exile* (*Israel Potter*) (1855), takes
a more ferocious pleasure in a similar idea; asked if he would
"strike" his colors to the *Serapis,* he replies "Aye!—I strike
back."[6] It is Ahab threatening to strike the sun if it insults him.
Probably he would use a harpoon to do it, and the skill of a
harpooneer. Melville, it seems, would use a pen and the craft of
a writer to strike back at enemies we shall later try to identify.
But here it is important to note that the word "craft" is to be
taken as both skill and deceitfulness. For in *The Confidence-
Man* the reader is the victim of a con man with (to quote Mark
Twain again) a "pen warmed up in hell." When he seems to
take the reader into his confidence, à la Fielding, Melville does
it not so much to settle as to raise questions and dilemmas of judgment. What these ambiguities are, who the confidence man is,
and how he is used in a book devoted to him, will be the subjects
of the rest of this discussion.

My purpose is not systematically to provide a key to the masks
of the confidence man. This has been done with imagination and
due deliberation by Elizabeth Foster as editor of the standard
edition of the work. It has also been done, with a more recon-
dite scholarship and an impressive air of finality, by H. Bruce
Franklin in *The Wake of the Gods*—an examination into the
comparative mythology behind Melville's works. Both critics
share a general belief that the confidence man is the incarnation
of a supernatural being or beings, using the slogans of a savior
god to effect the purposes of a devil. In the interests of general
orientation, I should say that I accept the high probability and
certainly the plausibility of Franklin's argument; he claims that
a pattern based on the avatars of the Hindu god Vishnu underlies the structure of *The Confidence-Man.* Yet, while accepting
this hypothesis as a useful way of ordering the events and characters, and of suggesting the large-scale religious implications of
the book, I do not find it useful beyond a certain point for eluci-

6. Herman Melville, *Israel Potter* (New York: Russell and Russell,
1963), p. 171.

dating what may be of sympathetic rather than mainly intellectual interest in the book. It identifies the masks but does not show us the face behind them, nor can it therefore suggest the expression worn by that face.

As I have stressed before, the confidence man as such has certain qualifications as a character in fiction. He is most obviously suited to be an instrument of satire, for he is sensitive to the outer forms of society. In particular his occupation gives him a quick ear for the rhetoric of human intercourse. For a moment withholding comment on the deaf-mute and the Cosmopolitan, I should like to suggest how the other six confidence men ape the sounds of optimism, tempting the listener to embrace a cherished hope which turns out to be a spike aimed at his breast. In each case I shall begin with an aspect of the common man's faith, and then go on to show how the confidence man makes use of, and thereby invalidates, that trust.

1. *Oppression and ill fortune can be mitigated, perhaps even transformed into a spiritual good, by an attitude of cheerful resignation and patient endurance.* Such, at least, is the motto of the true Christian. Black Guinea offers the specific example of the crippled and stunted Negro cheerfully accepting his knee-bent position in a pre–Civil War society, asking merely indulgence and charity for his real and figurative lowliness. The tone and diction of his appeal to "all you kind ge'mmen" is such as to reinforce the impression that humility softens a man's nature. But the underside of this language is prickly indeed. If one extends "massa," or master, to its ultimate reference on the same cosmic plane as the hot, baking sun, then the fact that Guinea is a "dog widout massa," depending on the "baker" sun for warmth, is tantamount to putting him in isolation from God. Summer with its warmed pavements is bearable; but winter is too awful to speak of. Guinea, as "the black sheep" (i.e., as Negro and as outcast from God's flock), craves warmth from the white sheep, but does so in vain. Finally, by introducing the later confidence men as "ge'mmen," he brackets them with the masters who promise what they do not mean to perform. Like the God who "loves" sufferers, they offer at most a brief season of hope.

2. *The overture of goodwill is its own proof of good credit, and lastingly endears the giver to the receiver.* Ringman, the con-

fidence man who follows Black Guinea, seems to believe that the memory of a friendship leaves an indelible impression. But does it? Ringman soothingly provides the urbane chatter of renewed acquaintanceship, asking Mr. Roberts, whom he has just recently accosted, whether he does not remember a friendly afternoon they once spent together. "Have you forgotten about the urn, and what I said about Werter's Charlotte, and the bread and butter, and the capital story you told of the large loaf."[7] It would seem ungracious at the least to deny a memory so gently coaxed forth, especially when it is hinted that to forget it would be to give proof of a loss of identity. The confidence man, who had previously purloined one of Mr. Roberts's business cards, now hands it to him with the suggestion that if Mr. Roberts does not know his old friend Mr. Ringman, then he does not know himself, and had better learn who he is from the name on the card. On board the *Fidèle* the truth is that names and identities are mere assertions, printed placards and a distinctive dress that label a man for the nonce. So it is not surprising that Mr. Roberts should hesitate and at last surrender his own faith in himself at the insistence of Mr. Ringman. But it does suggest the heresy that identity is mutable, and that memory is a matter of present expedient. In fact, after receiving a loan from Mr. Roberts, the confidence man's "manner assumed a kind and degree of decorum which, under the circumstances, seemed almost coldness" (*CM*, p. 23). It seems as though Mr. Ringman's own memory of a kindness is rapidly fading into the blank presented by stranger to stranger.

3. *Business principles, technological methods, and democratic procedures are adequate to the solution of all moral problems.* This, Melville seems to say, is another hope fondled by the American in particular. Why is it not possible for charity to pay monthly dividends, for inventions to cure malaise, and for misery to be outvoted? Thus saith the confidence man. The Agent for the Seminole Widow and Orphan Asylum is also the planner of a worldwide charity scheme. Says he, "Missions I would quicken with the Wall Street spirit" (*CM*, p. 35). He is also akin to the inventor as folk hero: "I invented my Protean easychair in odd

7. Herman Melville, *The Confidence-Man: His Masquerade*, ed. Hershel Parker (New York: W. W. Norton & Company, 1971), p. 15.

intervals stolen from meals and sleep" (*CM*, p. 33). The poor in London he would save by what sounds like a Congressional appropriation: "I am for voting to them twenty thousand bullocks and one hundred thousand barrels of flour to begin with" (*CM*, p. 35). Perhaps the last three words are the epitome of reckless optimism, the "hot air" of the talker as plenipotentiary. The absurdity of these schemes is patent; not so obvious is the fact that they caricature beliefs that are almost as extravagant, yet are seriously and deeply held by the average citizen of Melville's America.

4. *The land holds the power of regeneration and salvation.* Natural resources, like the coal of the Black Rapids Coal Company, and newly developed real estate, like the New Jerusalem for which Mr. Truman also sells stock—both are the sort of investment that involves faith in the land and its future. How disconcerting to learn that only a freak of the market makes the coal stock worth buying; how dampening to discover that the new town exists maybe only on paper, and that the city planner seems to have erected a perpetual fountain but no houses to live in. Mr. Truman's spiel describing the New Jerusalem seems almost a premonition of Colonel Sellers' affectionate creation of the city at Stone's Landing. Making use of a similar rhetoric, Mr. Truman holds forth: "There—there, you see are the public buildings—here the landing—there the park—yonder the botanic gardens—and this, this little dot here, is a perpetual fountain, you understand. You observe there are twenty asterisks. Those are for the lyceums. They have lignum-vitae rostrums" (*CM*, p. 43). But here even the enthusiasm is hollow. What we have is a travesty of the spirit that saw its future in towns spread across the country.

5. *Faith in a Christian Nature will cure ills of the body and spirit.* Under the more elaborate and more familiar spiel of the herb-doctor, we find this broader and more explicitly doctrinaire principle. Believe, and you will be cured, cries the medicine man:

Ladies and gentlemen, I hold in my hand here the Samaritan Pain Dissuader, thrice-blessed discovery of that disinterested friend of humanity whose portrait you see. Pure vegetable extract. Warranted to remove the acutest pain within less than ten minutes. Five hundred dollars to be forfeited on failure. Especially efficacious in heart disease and tic-douloureux. Observe the expression of this pledged friend of humanity. Price only fifty cents. (*CM*, p. 71–72)

It is of course Christ being offered at a premium. Some of the listeners are impervious to the herb-doctor's rhetoric; some resent him as a cruel raiser of hopes that must eventually be dashed; others cling to his words as to the breath of life. The colloquy that takes place after his forced retreat from the ship's ante-cabin suggests that this confidence man is more fool than knave or, rather, that he is a "a fanatic quack; essentially a fool, though effectively a knave" (*CM*, p. 76). And also a "genius." Probably the most trustworthy judgment on his real character is made by a man who defends his own insights by claiming that "true knowledge comes but by suspicion or revelation" (*CM*, p. 78). By these lights, which remind us of Ishmael's "doubts of all things earthly, and intuitions of some things heavenly," the passenger in question decides that the herb-doctor is a Jesuit emissary in disguise. And so he is, if we expand the term to read emissary of the Society of Jesus, and if we further grant that term its very broadest application. The herb-doctor appeals to all who believe implicitly in salvation by faith.

6. *Under favorable conditions, such as exist in America, every man will develop into a physically and morally sound being.* A principle much like this is upheld by the Philosophical Intelligence Office representative. Furthermore, the P.I.O. man claims that the special researches of his employment office amply support the most optimistic rendering of the national belief. The misanthropic Pitch is finally induced to yield to his real desire to believe in man's natural goodness and its healthy prospects in a healthy land. Though he has been disillusioned with thirty-five boys, the last having been chosen from among "the flowers of all nations, . . . temporarily in barracks on an East River island" (*CM*, p. 101), he is at last persuaded to venture his trust once again. America, the haven for the immigrant, is in a sense a vast employment office which confidently believes that the incomparable opportunities it offers will bring out the good in every man it adopts. And, should any specimen prove faulty, but give it time and its faults will be replaced by sound virtues. And so saying, the confidence man takes his departure at a landing significantly called the Devil's Joke.

Melville, as we have been seeing, uses the confidence man's gift for imitative styles of speech, his keen knowledge of the dearest hopes and beliefs of the average person, in order to play a kind of devil's joke on the reader. The feelings we would clutch at turn to nettles in our hands. Yet each is a common, ordinary sort of hope, the kind which is the daily bread of many lives (or so Melville would have us believe). The rarer, or more exquisite, sort of hope is the portion of the rarer and more exquisite sensibility; it is involved more intimately with the special characteristics of Melville's personality. These hopes also play a part in *The Confidence-Man*, and to define them it is helpful to consider another inherent quality of the confidence man. As a dramatic embodiment of the confusion between appearances and reality, he is ideally suited to act out the fantasies of a mind obsessed with this ancient dilemma.

By the time we reach *The Confidence-Man* in the sequence of Melville's work, we are prepared to say without too much hesitation that a fair, cajoling appearance is always a cover-up for an ugly, a brutal, or a sublimely indifferent reality. In the valley of the Typees a man may smile and smile and be a cannibal. The more sportive Omoo delightfully describes his sailing vessel, only to add, "but after all, Little Jule was not to be confided in. Lively enough, and playful she was, but on that very account the more to be distrusted."[8] Redburn, aboard a ship for the first time, is shocked to learn that the dockside manners of his captain are in no way like his insolence at sea. And White Jacket arrives at the further revelation that the clean, dry decks of a man-o'-war form the lid on a sink of iniquity. A deepening, widening menace accompanies the grace of Moby Dick at rest: "No wonder there had been some among the hunters who namelessly transported and allured by all this serenity, had ventured to assail it; but had fatally found that quietude but the vesture of tornadoes. Yet calm, enticing calm, oh whale! thou glidest on, to all who for the first time eye thee, no matter how many in that same way thou may'st have bejuggled and destroyed before."[9] And finally, in *Pierre*, Melville tells us that "a smile is the chosen

8. *Omoo*, p. 10.
9. *Moby-Dick*, ed. Harrison Hayford and Hershel Parker (New York: W. W. Norton & Company, 1967), pp. 447–48.

vehicle for all ambiguities." [10] Man is indeed capable of diabolical cheats, if one may judge by *Benito Cereno*, in which Babo,
that incarnation of evil, masquerades his reign of terror as a
peaceful day aboard ship.

In reviewing these examples of fairness belied and grace be-
deviled, one cannot help sensing a disillusionment that begins
as a small stain but spreads to discolor the universe. It is usually
believed that Melville's adolescent experience with the effects
of bankruptcy and the death of a father gave him his bitter distrust of apparent well-being. His early prosperity, like Redburn's,
gulled him by raising false hopes, and the relative failure of his
later books no doubt encouraged this feeling. It permeates *The
Confidence-Man*, where the main character sheathes his malice
in a scabbard of smiling benignity.

Then, too, the confidence man is inherently suited to the
demonstration of another of Melville's private persuasions. By
his power to manipulate the appearances worn by reality, he is
able to embody the notion that inconsistency is an important
characteristic of the human personality. We know that Melville
believed that it was. For example, in the aftermath of an affectionate enthusiasm contained in a letter to Hawthorne, Melville
warns him that if he posts an answering letter, he "will missend
it—for the very fingers that now guide this pen are not precisely
the same that just took it up and put it on this paper. Lord,
when shall we be done changing?" [11] The answer is that we shall
never cease being a stranger to ourselves, though we do not always change our clothes and our name when this happens. The
confidence man usually does. For the various disguises in which
he appears represent the empirically distinguishable and apparently unrelated expressions of a comprehensive but single mind.

As he may separate himself from yesterday's name, so he may
separate himself from yesterday's act. In his predatory role the
confidence man is normally independent of the social nexus of
community, family, and permanent friends, in short all relationships in which confidence depends, as it usually does, on long
association and proven experience. Figuratively speaking, the

10. *Pierre*, p. 84.
11. Melville, *The Letters of Herman Melville*, ed. Merrell R. Davis and
William H. Gilman (New Haven: Yale University Press, 1960), p. 142.

confidence man must build his Rome in a day so that he may be gone tomorrow. He is active in society but not responsible to it. Therefore, he is the ideal subject for a study which, the better to examine the connection, would artificially separate an act from its consequences, or a type of behavior from its final reward or punishment. Under these conditions it is possible to achieve, as I think Melville does, a new perspective on the relationship between a man and his worth to society. Here again I think Melville is chafing under what were for him the gallingly inappropriate maxims of his republic. There are two that in particular aggravate his resentment; the first provides us with a final way of looking at the six confidence men already mentioned, and the second helps us, perhaps, to understand why we both like and distrust the Cosmopolitan.

1. *Diligent, self-reliant effort, especially effort intended to benefit one's countrymen, will be materially rewarded in cash and prestige.* What might be called the Yankee-Puritan tradition in America underlies this concept; Benjamin Franklin is its validation. That Melville's own attitude toward this assumption was bitter and ironic we know. He was too proud to be entirely facetious when he told Hawthorne, "Though I wrote the Gospels in this century, I should die in the gutter." [12] *Israel Potter* is one long record of a patriot who deserved everything and got nothing from his country. Intended to be doubly ironic is the fact that in this book Benjamin Franklin, whose spirit is distilled in the motto "God helps those who help themselves," is partially unwilling and finally unable to help a man who risks everything to help his country. In *The Confidence-Man* Melville is less direct but just as bitter. He forces us into the awkward position of having to judge the confidence men against our inclinations or else modify our approval of the way in which we distribute rewards.

Three of the confidence men make their appeal on the basis of their own or another's undeserved misery or innocent victimization. Black Guinea, for one, is the victim of his color and what might be considered (with malice aforethought) as an "act of God" resulting in his deformity. No less bizarre is the case of Mr. Ringman, who is the victim of the undeserved and inexplica-

12. Ibid., p. 129.

ble malice of Goneril (there are of course hints here of the paranoia found in "I and My Chimney"). Finally, the agent of the Seminole Widows and Orphans reminds us of the disappropriation and ravage of the war in Florida. The victims exist, even if the relief society does not. In retrospect we find we can agree with Egbert (that need is always a punishment for culpable weakness) *only* if we are insensible to the pathos in the life of a Black Guinea, the agony borne by a husband of Goneril, and the desolation felt by the victims of war—that is to say, only if we dismiss the confidence man as a totally ineffectual sham with no real connection with our lives. It would seem that if we make this judgment, we stand condemned by our own inhumanity.

The next three con men make their appeal on the basis of special services offered, or of especially valuable products for sale. The transfer agent for the coal company, Mr. Truman, offers a rare chance at a propitious moment for the investor to "get in on" the future of his country; the herb-doctor offers a panacea in a bottle; and the P.I.O. man offers a guaranteed specimen of morally high-grade humanity. They ask us not to help them but to help ourselves. Incidentally, of course, we shall be keeping them in business. But we can agree that these men really deserve acknowledgment and reward *only* if we are insensible to the patently "phony" character of their wares—that is to say, only if we accept the confidence men as fully reliable benefactors of the human race, and in effect deny that they are confidence men at all. But we can hardly do this. Indeed, it would seem as impossible to take the P.I.O. man seriously as to take Black Guinea frivolously. To do so would be to admit that we are fools. And so we are left with the task of evaluating, in the case of each of these six avatars of the confidence man, exactly how much Melvillean truth he reveals on the surface and how much he hides underneath. Taken all together, the con men do have one voice, and it inversely hints that a man either gets less than he deserves, or more. To Melville it must have seemed that, in the matter of a man's claim on the purse of his countryman, justice was rarely done. Had he himself not served his country as valuably as Israel Potter, and had he not been neglected by the moral heirs of Ben Franklin?

2. *In human intercourse, the aggressive, practical, organiza-*

tional, materially productive qualities are more valuable (and hence to be rewarded more highly) than the yielding, luxuriating, appreciative, aesthetically productive qualities. This is a belief not so much Yankee-Puritan as Western industrial, in the sense that, for example, Twain's Hank Morgan is actually a child of the Western spirit but a product of industrial training. Now this is not the time to argue, as perhaps one should, that the first set of qualities here described is desirable in the world of affairs, the second in the world of art, and that the two should be kept clearly distinct. Melville, the artist, did feel unjustly humbled in the world of affairs. This bitterness, justified or unjustified, is relevant to our discussion here. And I believe his attitude toward this assumption is further complicated by a duality in his own nature, one which is often described as a commingling of masculine and feminine impulses but which is perhaps better thought of as a rhythm of defiance and submission. Undoubtedly he was capable of battering the world in a morose distemper, capable of creating figures who dominatingly assert a highly conscious ego through violent action. But certainly no one who remembers the Mardian pipe scenes, the letters to Hawthorne, or the night spent with Queequeg can doubt that Melville was also capable of an obverse tenderness, an indulgent mood of permissive yielding, a slipping away of the self into the sharp ecstasy and sweet languor of sensual repose, speculative thought, and the communion of an idealized friendship. In answer to what he saw as a materialistic and predatory spirit, he offered the shared couch, the genial bottle, and the fraternal pipe.

In dealing with the Cosmopolitan, we should remember the history of Melville's relationship to those beings who draw out the softened tendencies, to those beings whom he calls the "man-charmers." Marnoo of *Typee* may be the first of them. Gracious, godlike, a "Polynesian Apollo," "this all-attractive personage" wanders freely among various hostile tribes officially protected by the fact that he has a friend in every camp. He charms and palliates, but perhaps ultimately deceives. Taking up the life of a rover himself, Melville adopts the name describing such a taboo traveler and calls himself Omoo. Taji, in *Mardi*, is a more extreme and complicated rendering of man as a "strolling divinity." He becomes a god in order to save his life as a man; but the sin he committed as a man (the murder of a priest) he must expiate in a godly grandeur and in the godly isolation of eternity. Again on a human scale the powerful attractiveness of Harry Bolton wins the heart of Redburn and makes a docile worshiper of him. Putting on fake moustache and whiskers for the occasion, Bolton spirits him to London and introduces him into a mysterious building where an ineffable iniquity breathes through a luxuriant elegance. Redburn is both fascinated and repelled. Something of the same feeling can be seen in Melville's attitude toward master-at-arms Bland in *White Jacket*: "There was a fine polish about his whole person, and a pliant, insinuating style in his conversation, that was, socially, quite irresistible."[13] The same might be said of the Cosmopolitan. Melville describes Bland further: ". . . he blandly smiled, politely offered his cigar-holder to a perfect stranger, and laughed and chatted to right and left, as if springy, buoyant, and elastic, with an angelic conscience, and sure of kind friends wherever he went, both in this life and the life to come."[14] Again, we might be reading of the Cosmopolitan. Melville adds finally, "who can forever resist the very Devil himself, when he comes in the guise of a gentleman, free, fine, and frank?" Who, indeed, can resist Frank Goodman? Melville's own reaction to Bland offers an interesting suggestion of his feelings in creating the Cosmopolitan: "I, for one, regarded this master-at-arms with mixed feelings of detestation, pity, admiration, and something opposed to enmity. I could not but abominate him when I thought of his conduct [flagrant smuggling]; but I pitied the continual gnawing which, under all his deftly donned disguises, I saw lying at the bottom of his soul."[15] Whatever lies at the bottom of the Cosmopolitan's soul, it is something for which Melville has a sympathetic understanding. Like Twain's admiration for Charles Williams, the burglar who forges his own letter of recommendation, Melville's interest in the Cosmopolitan is based on a sort of fascinated respect for a man who has arranged to live with evil as the universal reality.

13. *White Jacket: or The World in a Man-of-War* (Evanston, Ill. and Chicago: Northwestern University Press and The Newberry Library, 1970), p. 187.
14. Ibid.
15. Ibid.

The Cosmopolitan, then, combines the gracious immunity of a traveling god and the warm sociability of the devil as gentleman. Conversationalist, convivialist, idealist, charmer of men, he is contrasted with the deaf-mute who comes aboard the *Fidèle* on April Fools' Day. In many ways the two are diametrically opposed to each other: the lamblike man is unfit for conversation and is dressed in a simple white suit; the Cosmopolitan is by occupation a talker and is dressed in a fantasia of colors and styles. The deaf-mute opens the book, and the Cosmopolitan closes it. Yet they are similar in certain respects, too. Both hail from distant lands and show the physical and mental signs of much travel. Both are interested in ideal principles and engage in no real transfers of cash, although the Cosmopolitan does give a token sum to Egbert and the mad poet (Melville patronizing Emerson and Poe!). It would seem as though the deaf-mute has the purity of the abstract thought, while the Cosmopolitan has the richness of the concrete deed.

More fully developed is the complementary relationship between the Cosmopolitan and Pitch. One is a "genial misanthrope," the other a "surly philanthropist." And here, if we may keep in mind what has been said of the rhythm of defiance and submission in Melville himself, we may find a way of getting behind the masquerade. But to do so it is necessary to stop and consider Pitch and the Cosmopolitan in the light of a fable that Melville rewrote more than once. Let us call it the fable of the Bear and the Fiddler. If it were to be set down in its essentials, it might read something like this:

Alone in a forest lived a Bear. His fur was thick and long to protect him from the unkind elements. His talons were curved and sharp to protect him from the rabid wolf. His grunt was deep and harsh.

In a clearing in the wood he came upon an upright figure whose limbs were lithe and delicate, whose robe was scaled and glistening, and who made music like a god.

Charmed by the spell of the Fiddler, the Bear sank down in a trance. His eyelids closed very slowly. When they opened, the clearing was empty.

If one now remembers the short story "The Fiddler," one can see how these themes parallel Melville's despair as a writer. The hero of this story, whose poem has just been torn apart by the wolfish critics, is introduced to the cheerful Hautboy. It appears that this mysterious man was once a great violinist who now fiddles country airs and lives a life of quiet pleasures and loving friends. Hearing him, the ruffled poet yields to "the bow of an enchanter," saying that "my whole splenetic soul capitulated to the magical fiddle. . . . And I, the charmed Bruin."[16] In *The Confidence-Man* the herb-doctor addresses the daughter of a huge and growling backwoodsman with the playful verse: "Hey diddle, diddle, the cat and the fiddle." With these very words, Poe had introduced his comic piece called, "Diddling Considered as One of the Exact Sciences." He, too, associated the fiddler with Jeremy Diddler, the archetypal swindler.[17] And here, enraged by the herb-doctor's claims that his medicine can heal the heart's woe, Melville's bearish titan cries out, "Profane fiddler on heart-strings! Snake!" (CM, p. 75) In the contrast of these two lines lies much of the ambiguity of the Cosmopolitan. Later, in describing himself as opposed to the "ursine Pitch," the Cosmopolitan explains that "the genial misanthrope [unlike Pitch, the surly philanthropist] will be a new kind of monster . . . he will take steps, fiddle in hand, and set the tickled world a' dancing" (CM, p. 154). Melville's attitude toward the fiddler is compounded of two mutually disturbing elements, the wishful yielding of the "charmed Bruin" and the clear perception that the music, since it cannot be genuine, must be a trick of the Devil. Melville allows the Cosmopolitan to admit, as perhaps he is himself admitting, that "a good fellow, singing a good song . . . woos forth my every spike, so that my whole hull, like a ship's sailing by a magnetic rock, caves in with acquiescence. Enough: when one has a heart of a certain sort, it is in vain trying to be resolute" (CM, p. 138). These words are Melville's answer to the opposing credo of the Western spirit.

What actually does the man-charmer do? He asks for a loan on the basis of friendship. By doing so, he establishes need as something different from the craven admission that Egbert believes it to be. Rather it ought to be, says the Cosmopolitan, a

16. Melville, *The Complete Stories of Herman Melville*, ed. Jay Leyda (New York: Random House, 1949), p. 239.
17. Cf. A. E. Senter, *The Diddler* (New York: M. Doolady, 1968).

bond which draws people toward a sense of community. It should be transformed, he implies, from a symbol of material giving to a symbol of emotional sharing. His effort to accomplish this is frustrated by Charles Arnold Noble's meanness of spirit and Mark Winsome's coldness of theory. Actually, what the Cosmopolitan offers is not a plea for charity or a product for sale—but only his richly faceted humanity, with all its multiform mystery. Thus he is clearly on a different plane from the confidence men who precede him; like them he is ambiguous in his moral effect, but he outdoes the most affecting of them with his appeal for "help, help, Charlie, I want help!" and goes beyond the most cruel of them in sweetening his venom. What he does is to dramatize finally and fully the beauty and the impossibility of a guileless human relationship.

Despite the interest we feel in the Cosmopolitan, we cannot help missing the presence in this book of a clearly defined personality. We hear no voice capable of echoing Ahab's boast: "In the midst of the personified impersonal, a personality stands here." Rather we have the refractions of a personality which fit together only on the level of ideas. As readers we are left with only the hint of an indefinable poignancy, a something which rouses our sympathy even though we are at a loss for an object to which it may properly be given. And in this condition we must remain, unless we grant Melville his right to be bitter against God. If we do, then perhaps we must give our sympathy to *him*, for he alone humanizes the book.

Only the most naive criticisms of *The Confidence-Man* have asserted that it ultimately and unequivocably affirms the validity and the value of the deaf-mute's appeal for universal charity. In the previous discussion I have tried to show that Melville was disenchanted with certain assumptions of a booming and blustering "new" country. But, as I hope I have also shown, he was a man singularly vulnerable to enchantments of another kind, to softenings and yearnings which the most brutal treatment could not drive from his affections, but which were nevertheless too bruised and tender for unprotected exposure. American men did not say such things openly. Perhaps, then, they could only be said under the thick disguise of an obvious joke.

After a full realization of the con man's diabolical mission and

Melville's bitterest cynicism, it may be possible to say that the role of the confidence man works two ways in this book. Melville has made a hero of the Devil in order to expose his adamantine malice against the premises of a Christian industrial society; perhaps he has also made a devil of his hero in order to hide a nationally inadmissable but personally indispensable allegiance to the true sentimentalist. For Melville, another easily wounded "misanthropic philanthropist," the confidence man offered a needed protection, a mirrored shield, the ultimate mask from behind which an embattled author could address his country.

The Fictive Imagination as a "Useful Art"

We are in a sense victims of the surrender of the James River to the Charles. John Smith of Jamestown was a man who saw marvels and thought dramas, always with himself as the hero. In this role he approximated the Elizabethan ideal, for his deeds were the index to the visions of his mind and his books were the acts for which his life was renowned. For him as for Ovid Bolus, all ideas were facts. It is difficult to tell, for example, just how much of the Pocahontas story is history and how much is an Elizabethan tall tale. A certain romantic license of invention might have developed earlier into a national habit if it had not been for the reasons of conscience that made the Pilgrims decline the services of John Smith as a guide.

On the chilly isle of Shawmut the blend of fact and fiction seems not to have been so characteristic as the mixture of piety and commerce. In Boston ingenuity was absorbed in the problems of economic enterprise and religious controversy. A random fit of imagination such as the heresy of Anne Hutchinson was summarily condemned. One gets the impression that a terrible efficiency bent all thoughts and all activities to the furtherance of God's kingdom on earth; and a good deal of attention was paid to the shocking waste of sainthood in the hypocrite. The Puritan saw the hypocrite as a man who lived a godly life on the surface but did not feel a true commitment to God. We must remember the Calvinist paradox that good works have no effect on a man's spiritual destiny—although they are the sign by which his holiness is known. Inevitably, in a community where spiritual worth is the most important social advantage, it is going to be a matter of practical wisdom to appear virtuous even if one is not. One legacy of the Charles River culture is that, whatever a man's private conviction, he must satisfy the deacons of the world, he must prove a useful member of society. Translated into the crudest terms, this is the requirement that a man put his energies to work in a practical way and that he at least appear to benefit others at the same time.

Even the imported Cambridge graduate presumably knew how to milk a cow. The conditions of frontier life—and there was a frontier somewhere for many years—continually rewarded "useful" knowledge and punished the lack of it. The special quality of practical piety and canny wisdom we associate with a certain type of New Englander, the storied Yankee, is of Puritan descent. In a more specific context American inventiveness in the mechanical arts is almost proverbial and was considered to be the channel into which all our initiative poured, leaving that of imaginative or fine art very narrow and dry. This is an old complaint and a constant one throughout the nineteenth century. We have little respect for the man who lives only in his mind; we have a great deal of respect for the man who is active in affairs and can show us the rewards of his talent. In other words, we prefer the Puritan hypocrite who has a cow and a barn to the idle dreamer who has only ideas. Hawthorne sensed this and was chagrined; Melville saw it and was resentful. Every writer knew it and reacted according to his temperament. I would suggest that one fruitful way of regarding the confidence man character is as a storyteller who must also be practical. We should keep in mind the conditions attached to the exercise of the imagination in America. In certain cases a mind richly peopled with characters and dramas, yet guided by a wholly material ambition and governed by a pragmatic conscience, might very well fit one for the career of a confidence man. It was one way of making a living from one's imagination. In the foregoing chapters I have tried to show the affinity between the literary mind and the mind of the confidence man. I would now suggest, by way of summary and review, that the confidence man illustrates the fictive imagination employed as a "useful art."

Returning to the backwoods where this study began, we come again to the "original" character. For Simon Suggs, as for the hunters who preceded him, the practical morality is simply one of self-preservation. There are no values to put in the balance against the obvious virtue of making every situation pay. One must not forget the effects of mere newness of experience. New terrain, new climate, new modes of life suggest, inspire, and sometimes demand practical inventiveness on the part of those who live by their wits. "In a new country . . . ," says Suggs, one has to adjust, adapt, be "shifty." By way of special endowment he is gifted with the fiction-maker's eye and ear. He understands the diction, opinions, and characteristic poses of his fellow men so well that he can cast himself in the roles of captain, preacher, or congressman at will. In an older English atmosphere and without the binding American need to "do something," this practical psychologist might have become a writer of satirical essays or comic plays. In Kentucky, he acts out his farce on the stage of real life—and makes his living in the process.

In an earlier chapter I described the confidence man as someone who had personalized the concept of manifest destiny. During a period of rapid territorial and financial growth, the confidence man simply applies to himself the view that opportunity carries its own moral sanction. The only limits to aggrandizement are obdurate physical barriers. One need not stop short of the Pacific Ocean; one need not stop short of the hangman's noose. Considering the whole atmosphere of puffed ventures and bubble schemes that really paid off, we should recognize that the American imagination was fully alive at a time when material gain was the nation's motto. The con man here is an individual whose imagination is not tied to a long-term work ethic, but is tied to an active spirit of adventure and acquisition. He learns the very useful art of what Mark Twain calls "spreading" himself, or what we might call "self-promotion." Where the backwoods hunter relies on physical prowess to trap his victim, the con man of the midcentury relies on rhetoric. He is typically itinerant and the world presents itself to him as a succession of audiences he is challenged to persuade. Men and women and often crowds of men and women are his acreage and his gold mine. His competitive advantage is all of those things that give one man a psychological edge over another—intelligence, a fluent tongue, powers of ingratiation and personal magnetism. No one understood better than Mark Twain the power of words in a democracy. As we have seen, Twain's confidence men are masters of the evangelical tradition and instinctively take into account the inbred respect for a pulpit. The related tradition of political oratory is equally familiar to them. They use a platform as another man uses a horse—to get where they want to go. It is hardly necessary to add that the popular press was an ersatz platform and that both literary hoaxes and P. T. Barnum's advertisements were very much in the tradition of the tall tale and the "pitch-man's" harangue. The doubtful veracity of the newspaper story was a standing joke, and the attitude of the more cultivated society can be seen in Cooper's description of a small-town editor in *Homeward Bound*: ". . . practice had made him intimately acquainted with all the frauds, deceptions, and vileness of the ordinary arts of paragraph-making. . . ."[1] One may think of such editors as having turned word-mongering into a very useful art.

In these and other confidence men we see a public ethic of industry or "business" in conflict with a private ideal of laziness—what Mark Twain called "sliding" and what Melville called "melting." These terms are both pejorative and alluring to the men who use them. One may imagine that Governor Winthrop of Boston would have had no difficulty in identifying a con man as the Devil. But the nineteenth-century appeal of the roving "man-charmer" is perhaps an instance of a subversive counter-mood, an alien orientalism or more accurately primitivism, something that wooed Emerson in his visions of radiant personalities, something that reached Twain through the Negro and Melville through the Polynesian. The opposite pull of the puritanic and the hedonistic is one aspect of the malaise suffered by these two writers. How can the idle life of the imagination be made to yield hard cash? The problem is ironically formulated and resolved in the person of an alter ego, the confidence man.

In the last quarter of the century the shift from an agricultural to an urban culture began to alter the *modus operandi* of the con man. In the middle of the city he was granted the anonymity which formerly he had had to achieve by moving from one village to the next. On a more sophisticated level now, the con game might involve making the right contacts. The problem

1. James Fenimore Cooper, *Homeward Bound* (New York: R. T. Fenno & Co., 1900), p. 195.

might be one of social entrée. This is the stage for the minor charlatans in Eggleston's *The Faith Doctor*; it is instinctive with a number of James's characters. The confidence man in the era of Andrew Carnegie is filled with the idea of personal empire. Rhetoric may still be instrumental to his power, but his distinguishing quality is the ability to use money (and social position) as a commodity or bargaining power. Perhaps if someone like Kate Croy has a moral pattern it is that of social Darwinism. She believes in the right of superior physical and mental force to exert itself at the expense of such weaker beings as Milly Theale. James's equation of her personal "desire" and her creative "intelligence" is another way of saying that her practical needs give her the plot for her imagination to develop.

It is difficult to draw a line at 1900 or even at James's death in 1916. Yet I have done so in this study because I see the confidence man as part of the nineteenth-century perspective on life in America. If the history of this character type were pursued into the twentieth century, the relation of the fictive imagination to current realities and to practical survival would change. No doubt Jay Gatsby is a pivotal figure here. F. Scott Fitzgerald created a person who becomes a confidence man primarily because of an overactive imagination coupled with an overactive ambition for the American ideal of success. But the posing of Jimmy Gatz as Gatsby is a different thing from the posing of Suggs as General Witherspoon, precisely because it is so much more innocent and passionate. It is also regressive. A decaying myth has infected Gatsby with a disease of the soul. The warrant of mere personality, which was the glory of the nineteenth-century man, has now become a lost dream rather than a fact which can be fictionalized. Gatsby does not see the 1920s clearly enough to be a successful confidence man.

In general the tendency of modern literature has been to depict the individual opposed by a monolithic array of forces that cooperate only with each other. The hero often begins with a loser's stance, as for example in Saul Bellow's *Seize the Day* and *Henderson the Rain King*. Merely to exist often takes more confidence than is available. Such an attitude annihilates the confidence man. Yet he may not be wholly extinct as a literary device. It may be that the literature of "black humor," which is generally considered existential in thought and absurdist in technique, has revived a mutant form of the con man. Once it is assumed that the world is irrational and even mad, then any coherent plan for survival is really a trick being played on those who take the world seriously. The heroes of Ken Kesey's *One Flew Over the Cuckoo's Nest* and Joseph Heller's *Catch-22* find it necessary to put on an antic disposition in order to save their individuality. This is a desperate ploy rather than a useful art.

Recently the genre of the literary hoax has been revived by Clifford Irving, who also seems to view himself as a kind of antihero at war with the Establishment. In the book in which he recounts his adventures as a literary con man,[2] he assumes that the world is absurd or "mad" and that therefore a "put-on" is a legitimate act of self-assertion. Many of the classical elements of the con game are still present: the affinity—in this case the identity—with literary fictionalizing; the skill in manufacturing emotionally colored personal detail; the superior understanding of the victim's weaknesses; the sense of personal drama and inspired creation. But in other ways the freakishness of this case only reminds us that the con man is no longer a salient and useful character in American fiction. The interplay of fantasy and fact, imagination and "real" or "useful" knowledge, has moved into such different arenas as science fiction. There the author himself is a richly tolerated con man, but he is normally not concerned, in a literary sense, with the implications of his role.

It is doubtful whether even a better writer than Irving could make critical use of the con man to show what is wrong with modern society or to express the relationship of the sensitive artist to an insensitive world. Perhaps the reason is that the onus of false credibility has been shifted too generally onto the large-scale organization—the army, the government, the community itself. The individual has become the last refuge of integrity, though he have but a pinpoint of honesty. If he has the fictive imagination, other things are required of it than that it be "useful" in getting him a living. More important, he is pointedly denied the full and reliable knowledge of life that is the *sine*

2. Clifford Irving, *What Really Happened: The Untold Story of the Hughes Affair* (New York: Grove Press, 1972).

qua non of the confidence man. Suggs and Twain's King and Frank Goodman are at ease in a world they understand too well; they are ideally suited to the purpose of the social critic who wants to point out the foibles of a youthful country. Today, having less credit to spare, we begin with a narrower margin of confidence. We are a little too apt to fear that we have been conned by the twentieth century.

Works Consulted

General

Bergmann, Johannes Dietrich. "The Original Confidence Man," *American Quarterly* 21 (Fall 1969): 560–77.

Blair, Walter. *Horse Sense in American Humor: From Benjamin Franklin to Ogden Nash*. Chicago: University of Chicago Press, 1952.

Boatright, Mody C. *The Sky is My Tipi*. Publications of the Texas Folklore Society, no. 22. Dallas: Southern Methodist University Press, 1949.

————, Wilson M. Hudson, and Allen Maxwell. *Texas Folk and Folklore*. Publications of the Texas Folklore Society, no. 26. Dallas: Southern Methodist University Press, 1954.

Boynton, Percy H. *The Rediscovery of the Frontier*. Chicago: The University of Chicago Press, 1931.

Brackenridge, Hugh Henry. *Modern Chivalry: Containing the Adventures of Captain John Farrago and Teague O'Regan, His Servant*, ed. Lewis Leary. New Haven: College and University Press, 1965.

Canby, Henry Seidel. *The Age of Confidence: Life in the Nineties*. New York: Holt, Rinehart & Winston, 1934.

Cook, Ebenezer. *The Sot-Weed Factor*. London: D. Bragg, 1708.

Cooper, James Fenimore. *Homeward Bound*. New York: R. T. Fenno & Co., 1900.

Davenport, Richard A. *Sketches of Imposture, Deception, and Credulity*. Philadelphia: G. B. Zieber & Co., 1845.

Dobie, Frank; Mody C. Boatwright; and Harry H. Ransom. *In the Shadow of History*. Texas Folklore Society Publications, no. 15. Hatboro, Pa.: Folklore Associates, Inc., 1966.

Garland, Hamlin. *Boy Life on the Prairie*, rev. ed. New York: Harper & Brothers, 1899.

Irving, Clifford. *What Really Happened: The Untold Story of the Hughes Affair*. New York: Grove Press, 1972.

Jones, Howard Mumford. *O Strange New World*. New York: The Viking Press, 1968.

Lynn, Kenneth S. *Mark Twain and Southwestern Humor*. Boston: Little, Brown & Company, 1959.
Meine, Franklin J. *Tall Tales of the Southwest*. New York: Alfred A. Knopf, 1930.
Rourke, Constance. *American Humor: A Study of the National Character*. New York: Harcourt, Brace & Co., 1931.
Senter, A. E. *The Diddler*. New York: M. Doolady, 1868.
Tanner, Tony. *The Reign of Wonder: Naivety and Reality in American Literature*. Cambridge, Eng.: Cambridge University Press, 1965.
Wister, Owen. "Quack-Novels and Democracy," *The American Monthly* 115 (June 1915): 721–34.

Chapter One: From the East

Baldwin, Joseph G. *The Flush Times of Alabama and Mississippi: A Series of Sketches*. New York: D. Appleton and Co., 1853.
Bonner, T. D. *The Life and Adventures of James P. Beckwourth*. New York: Harper & Brothers, 1856.
Cady, Edwin Harrison. *The Gentleman in America*. Syracuse: Syracuse University Press, 1949.
Cooper, James Fenimore. *The Deerslayer: Or, The First War Path*. 2 vols. Philadelphia: Lea and Blanchard, 1841.
———. *The Last of the Mohicans; A Narrative of 1757*. 3 vols. London: John Miller, 1826.
———. *Notions of the Americans: Picked up by a Travelling Bachelor*. 2 vols. London: Henry Colburn, 1828.
———. *The Pathfinder: Or, the Inland Sea*. 2 vols. Philadelphia: Lea and Blanchard, 1840.
———. *The Pioneers, or the Sources of the Susquehanna: A Descriptive Tale*. 2 vols. New York: Charles Wiley, 1823.
———. *The Prairie, A Tale*. 3 vols. Paris: Hector Bossange, 1827.
Crockett, David. *A Narrative of the Life of David Crockett, of the State of Tennessee*. Philadelphia: E. L. Carey and A. Hart, 1834.
———. *Sketches and Eccentricities of Col. David Crockett of West Tennessee*. New York: J. & J. Harper, 1883.
DeVoto, Bernard. *Mark Twain's America and Mark Twain at Work*. Boston: Houghton Mifflin Company, 1967.
Fiedler, Leslie A. *The Return of the Vanishing American*. New York: Stein and Day, 1968.
Flint, Timothy. *The First White Man of the West; or, the Life and Exploits of Col. Dan'l Boone, The First Settler of Kentucky*. Cincinnati: Morgan & Co., 1850.
Fussell, Edwin. *Frontier: American Literature and the American West*. Princeton: Princeton University Press, 1965.
Haliburton, Thomas Chandler. *The Clockmaker; of the Sayings and*

Doings of Samuel Slick of Slickville, 5th ed. 3 vols. London: Richard Bentley, 1839.

————. *The Letter Bag of the Great Western; or, Life in a Steamer.* London: Richard Bentley, 1840.

————. *Sam Slick,* ed. Ray Palmer Baker. New York: George H. Doran, 1923.

Harris, George Washington. *High Times and Hard Times.* Nashville: Vanderbilt University Press, 1967.

————. *Sut Lovingood Yarns.* New York: Dick & Fitzgerald, 1867.

Hoole, W. Stanley. *Alias Simon Suggs: The Life and Times of Johnson Jones Hooper.* University, Ala.: University of Alabama Press, 1952.

Hooper, Johnson Jones. *Some Adventures of Captain Simon Suggs.* Philadelphia: H.C. Baird, 1850.

Longstreet, Augustus B. *Georgia Scenes, Characters, Incidents, &c, in the First Half Century of the Republic,* 2nd ed. New York: Harper & Brothers, 1840.

————. *Stories with a Moral.* Philadelphia: John C. Winston Co., 1912.

Porter, William T., ed. *The Big Bear of Arkansas.* Philadelphia: Carey & Hart, 1845.

Robb, John S. *Streaks of Squatter Life, and Far-West Scenes.* Gainesville, Fla.: Scholars' Facsimiles and Reprints, 1962.

Williams, William Carlos. *In the American Grain.* New York: New Directions, 1956.

Chapter Two: To the West

Billington, Ray Allen. "The Origin of the Land Speculator as a Frontier Type," *Agricultural History* 19 (October 1945): 204–22.

Boatwright, Mody C. *Folk Laughter on the American Frontier.* New York: The Macmillan Co., 1949.

Boynton, Henry W. *Bret Harte.* New York: McClure, Phillips, & Co., 1908.

Cable, George W. *Old Creole Days.* New York: Charles Scribner's Sons, 1945.

Clappe, Louise Amelia K. [Dame Shirley]. *The Shirley Letters from the California Mines,* 1851–52. New York: Alfred A. Knopf, 1949.

Devol, George. *Forty Years a Gambler on the Mississippi,* 2nd ed. New York: George H. Devol, 1892.

Harte, Francis Brett. "Plain Language from Truthful James (the Heathen Chinee)." Pamphlet. Boston: James R. Osgood & Co., 1871.

————. *The Writings of Bret Harte.* 19 vols. Boston: Houghton Mifflin Company, 1896–1906.

Hazard, Lucy L. *The Frontier in American Literature.* New York: Barnes & Noble, 1941.

Lee, Robert Edson. *From West to East: Studies in the Literature of the American West.* Urbana: University of Illinois Press, 1966.

Paxson, Frederic Logan. *History of the Frontier, 1763–1893.* Boston: Houghton Mifflin Company, 1924.

Sealsfield, Charles. *Frontier Life: or, Tales of the South-Western Border.* New York: C. M. Sexton, 1859.

Shinn, M. W. "Cherokee Bob, the Original of Jack Hamlin," *The Overland Monthly* 68 (December 1916): 539–43.

Stoddard, Charles Warren. *In the Footprints of the Padres.* San Francisco: A. M. Robertson, 1902.

Walker, Franklin. *San Francisco's Literary Frontier.* New York: Alfred A. Knopf, 1939.

Chapter Three: And Back Again

Billington, Ray Allen. *America's Frontier Heritage.* New York: Holt, Rinehart & Winston, 1966.

Blair, Walter. *Mark Twain & Huck Finn.* Berkeley: University of California Press, 1960.

Clemens, Samuel Langhorne. *The Writings of Mark Twain.* 37 vols. New York: Gabriel Wells, 1922–25.

———. *The Autobiography of Mark Twain, Including Chapters Now Published for the First Time,* ed. Charles Neider. New York: Harper & Brothers, 1959.

Ferguson, De Lancey, "The Petrified Truth," *The Colophon News Series, A Quarterly for Bookmen,* 2, New Series (Winter 1937): 188–96.

Harrison, James G. "A Note on the Duke in 'Huck Finn': The Journeyman Printer as a Picaro," *Mark Twain Quarterly* 8 (Winter 1947): 1–2.

Howells, W. D. *Impressions and Experiences.* New York: Harper & Brothers, 1896.

———. *My Mark Twain.* New York and London: Harper & Brothers, 1910.

Marckwardt, Albert H. *American English.* New York: Oxford University Press, 1958.

Nott, Henry Junius. *Novelettes of a Traveller.* 2 vols. New York: Harper & Brothers, 1834.

Kaplan, Justin. *Mr. Clemens and Mark Twain: A Biography.* New York: Simon and Schuster, 1966.

Poe, Edgar Allan. *Complete Works of Edgar Allan Poe,* ed. James A. Harrison. 17 vols. New York: Fred De Fau and Co., 1902.

Whiting, B. J. "Guyuscutus, Royal Nonesuch and Other Hoaxes," *Southern Folklore Quarterly* 8 (December 1944): 251–75.

Chapter Four: From the Other World

Barnum, P. T. *The Humbugs of the World: An Account of Humbugs, Delusions, Impositions, Quackeries, Deceits and Deceivers Generally, in all Ages.* New York: Carleton Publisher, 1866.

Belcher, Hannah Graham. "Howells's Opinions on the Religious Conflicts of his Age as Exhibited in Magazine Articles," *American Literature* 15 (November 1943): 262–78.

Bell, Millicent. *Hawthorne's View of the Artist.* Albany: State University of New York, 1962.

Brooks, Van Wyck. *Howells, His Life and World.* New York: E. P. Dutton & Co., 1959.

Eggleston, Edward. *The Circuit Rider.* New York: Charles Scribner's Sons, 1903.

Gibson, William M., and George Arms. *A Bibliography of William Dean Howells.* New York: New York Public Library, 1948.

Hall, Lawrence Sargent. *Hawthorne, Critic of Society.* New Haven: Yale University Press, 1944.

Hawthorne, Nathaniel. *The Blithedale Romance and Fanshawe.* Columbus: The Ohio State University Press, 1964.

Hough, Robert Lee. *The Quiet Rebel: William Dean Howells as Social Commentator.* Lincoln: University of Nebraska Press, 1959.

Howells, W. D. *The Leatherwood God.* New York: The Century Co., 1916.

———. *The Undiscovered Country.* Boston: Houghton Mifflin Company, 1880.

McCabe, Joseph. *Spiritualism: A Popular History from 1847.* London: T. Fisher Unwin Ltd., 1920.

Male, Roy. *Hawthorne's Tragic Vision.* Austin: University of Texas Press, 1957.

Reed, Amy Louise. "Self-Portraiture in the Work of Nathaniel Hawthorne," *Studies in Philology* 23 (1926): 40–54.

Stein, William Bysshe. *Hawthorne's Faust, a Study of the Devil Archetype.* Gainesville: University of Florida Press, 1953.

Taneyhill, R. H. "The Leatherwood God. An Account of the Appearance and Pretensions of Joseph C. Dylks in Eastern Ohio in 1828," *Ohio Valley Historical Series,* Miscellanies, no. 7, pt. 3. Cincinnati: Robert Clark & Co., 1870.

Von Abele, Rudolph R. *The Death of the Artist; A Study of Hawthorne's Disintegration.* The Hague: Nijhoff, 1955.

Chapter Five: To the Old World

Anderson, Quentin. *The American Henry James.* New Brunswick, N. J.: Rutgers University Press, 1957.

Brooks, Van Wyck. *The Pilgrimage of Henry James.* New York: E. P. Dutton & Co., 1925.

Brown, Charles Brockden. *Wieland, or the Transformation. An American Tale* ... New York: T & J. Swords, 1798.

Canby, Henry Seidel. *Turn West, Turn East: Mark Twain and Henry James*. Boston: Houghton Mifflin Company, 1951.

Crews, Frederick C. *The Tragedy of Manners*. New Haven: Yale University Press, 1957.

Dietrichson, Jan W. *The Image of Money in the American Novel of the Gilded Age*. New York: Humanities Press, 1970.

James, Henry. *The Bostonians*. New York: Modern Library, 1956.

————. *Confidence*. London: The Macmillan Co., 1921.

————. *Daisy Miller and An International Episode*. New York: Harper & Brothers, 1892.

————. *The Golden Bowl*. 2 vols. London: The Macmillan Co., 1923.

————. *The Wings of the Dove*. 2 vols. New York: Charles Scribner's Sons, 1902.

————. *The Complete Tales of Henry James*, ed. Leon Edel. 12 vols. Philadelphia: J. B. Lippincott Co., 1962–65.

Matthiessen, F. O. *Henry James: The Major Phase*. New York: Oxford University Press, 1944.

Chapter Six: And Back to Melville

Anderson, Charles R. *Melville in the South Seas*. New York: Columbia University Press, 1939.

Arvin, Newton. *Herman Melville*. New York: The Viking Press, 1957.

Blackmur, R. P. "The Craft of Herman Melville," *The Virginia Quarterly Review* 14 (Spring 1938): 266–82.

Bowen, Merlin. *The Long Encounter: Self and Experience in the Writings of Herman Melville*. Chicago: University of Chicago Press, 1960.

Braswell, William. "Melville as a Critic of Emerson," *American Literature* 9 (November 1937): 317–34.

Chase, Richard V. *Herman Melville, A Critical Study*. New York: The Macmillan Co., 1949.

————. "Melville's *Confidence Man*," *The Kenyon Review* (Winter 1949): 122–40.

Curl, Vega. *Pasteboard Masks; Fact as Spiritual Symbol in the Novels of Hawthorne and Melville*. Cambridge, Mass.: Harvard University Press, 1931.

Drew, Philip. "Appearance and Reality in Melville's *The Confidence Man*," *Journal of English Language History* 31 (December 1964): 418–42.

Franklin, H. Bruce. *The Wake of the Gods: Melville's Mythology*. Stanford: Stanford University Press, 1963.

"Herman Melville's Confidence," *The Times Literary Supplement*, no. 2493 (November 11, 1949): 733.

Hetherington, Hugh W. *Melville's Reviewers*. Chapel Hill: The University of North Carolina Press, 1961.

Hoffman, Dan G. "Melville's 'Story of China Aster,' " *American Literature* 22 (May 1950): 137–49.

Karcher, Carolyn Lury. "The Story of Charlemont: A Dramatization of Melville's Concepts of Fiction in *The Confidence-Man: His Masquerade*," *Nineteenth-Century Fiction* 21 (June 1966): 73–84.

Levin, Harry. *The Power of Blackness*. New York: Alfred A. Knopf, 1958.

Mason, Ronald C. *Spirit Above the Dust: A Study of Herman Melville*. London: J. Lehmann, 1951.

Melville, Herman. *The Complete Stories of Herman Melville*, ed. Jay Leyda. New York: Random House, 1949.

———. *The Confidence-Man: His Masquerade*, ed. Hershel Parker. New York: W. W. Norton & Company, 1971.

———. *Israel Potter*. New York: Russell and Russell, 1963.

———. *The Letters of Herman Melville*, ed. Merrell R. Davis and William H. Gilman. New Haven: Yale University Press, 1960.

———. *Mardi: and A Voyage Thither*. Evanston, Ill., and Chicago: Northwestern University Press and The Newberry Library, 1970.

———. *Moby-Dick*, ed. Harrison Hayford and Hershel Parker. New York: W. W. Norton & Company, 1967.

———. *Omoo: A Narrative of Adventures in the South Seas*. Evanston, Ill., and Chicago: Northwestern University Press and The Newberry Library, 1968.

———. *Pierre: or The Ambiguities*. Evanston, Ill., and Chicago: Northwestern University Press and The Newberry Library, 1971.

———. *Typee: A Peep at Polynesian Life*. Evanston, Ill., and Chicago: Northwestern University Press and The Newberry Library, 1968.

———. *White Jacket: or The World in a Man-of-War*. Evanston, Ill., and Chicago: Northwestern University Press and The Newberry Library, 1970.

Metcalf, Eleanor M. *Herman Melville, Cycle and Epicycle*. Cambridge, Mass.: Harvard University Press, 1953.

Miller, Perry. *The Raven and the Whale*. New York: Harcourt, Brace & Co., 1956.

Mumford, Lewis. *Herman Melville*. New York: Harcourt, Brace & Co., 1929.

Oliver, Egbert S. "Melville's Picture of Emerson and Thoreau in 'The Confidence-Man,' " *College English* 8 (November 1946): 61–72.

Rosenberry, Edward H. *Melville and the Comic Spirit.* Cambridge, Mass.: Harvard University Press, 1955.

Sedgwick, William E. *Herman Melville: The Tragedy of Mind.* Cambridge, Mass.: Harvard University Press, 1944.

Thompson, Lawrance. *Melville's Quarrel with God.* Princeton: Princeton University Press, 1952.

Von Abele, Rudolph. "Melville and the Problem of Evil," *American Mercury* 65 (November 1947): 592–98.

Watters, R. E. "Melville's 'Isolatoes,' " *Publications of the Modern Language Association* 60 (December 1945): 1138–48.

Weaver, Raymond M. *Herman Melville: Mariner and Mystic.* New York: George H. Doran Co., 1921.

Index